LOYALIST REBELLION
IN NEW BRUNSWICK

A DEFINING CONFLICT FOR
CANADA'S POLITICAL CULTURE

With Thanks from the
International Law Society
undlaw Hall

David Bell
Feb 2014

LOYALIST REBELLION
IN NEW BRUNSWICK

A DEFINING CONFLICT FOR
CANADA'S POLITICAL CULTURE

DAVID BELL

FORMAC PUBLISHING COMPANY LIMITED
HALIFAX

Formac Publishing Company Limited recognizes the support of the Province of Nova
Scotia through the Department of Communities, Culture and Heritage. We are pleased
to work in partnership with the province to develop and promote our culture resources
for all Nova Scotians. We acknowledge the financial support of the Government of
Canada through the Canada Book Fund for our publishing activities. We acknowledge
the support of the Canada Council for the Arts which last year invested $157 million to
bring the arts to Canadians throughout the country.

Cover design: Meghan Collins
Cover image: iStock

Library and Archives Canada Cataloguing in Publication

Bell, D. G. (David Graham), 1953-, author
    Loyalist rebellion in New Brunswick / David Bell.

Includes bibliographical references and index.
ISBN 978-1-4595-0277-2 (pbk.)

    1. United Empire loyalists--Political activity--New Brunswick.
2. New Brunswick--Politics and government--1784-1867. 3. Canada--
Politics and government--1783-1791. 4. Political culture--Canada--
History. I. Title.

FC2471.3.B44 2013   971.5'102   C2013-904349-7

Formac Publishing Company Limited
5502 Atlantic Street
Halifax, Nova Scotia, Canada
B3H 1G4
www.formac.ca

Printed and bound in Canada.

CONTENTS

ACKNOWLEDGEMENTS

I began the research presented here at the suggestion of that legendary mentor of historians of eastern Canada, George Rawlyk (1935–95). It saw print first as *Early Loyalist Saint John* (1983). As I was preparing an expanded version of that book, James Lorimer suggested that the story of the suppression of political dissent in Loyalist New Brunswick deserved telling for a wider audience. I'm grateful for that suggestion, and for his willingness to publish the result. I'm also pleased to be able to thank students, friends and colleagues at the University of New Brunswick's Faculty of Law for their support over many years. If some of them have wondered whether constitutional history was really *law*, they've always been too polite to say so.

I am grateful to Ernest Clarke for the use of his map of Loyalist Saint John.

INTRODUCTION

Loyalist: One who professes uncommon adherence to his king.

Samuel Johnson, *Dictionary of the English Language* (1755)

Loyalty is a virtue. Yet somehow the title "Loyalist," when applied to historical groups, takes on awkward associations. Long before the world came to disdain the stubborn Protestant Loyalists of Ireland and the forlorn Republican Loyalists of 1930s Spain, the term was a label for those who showed uncommon adherence to the cause of king and empire in the American Revolution.

When Americans refer to Loyalists they mean those who resisted the break with Britain. They were the revolution's wretched losers and, for Americans, they disappear from view at war's end. But when Canadians refer to Loyalists they mean that subset of loyal Americans who fled northward into exile between 1782 and 1784. Their advent triggered the division of Quebec and Nova Scotia and from them the creation of New Brunswick, Cape Breton and Upper Canada. It was their arrival in the future Canada which determined that northern America would be shared by two nations rather than monopolized by one.

The Loyalists considered in this book are a band of some ten thousand adherents of the Crown who found themselves trapped in and around British-occupied New York City at the end of the Revolution. Rather than face renewed persecution by the victors, they chose exile to the St. John River region of what was then western Nova Scotia.

Almost from the day in May 1783 when the first fleet of shattered Loyalists reached St. John harbour from New York, many voiced bitter dissatisfaction with their new leadership. Vulnerable and sullen, they were quick to suspect those appointed to run the new settlements of manipulating government assistance so as to favour the few at the expense of the many. In this favouritism they saw a scheme to reduce them to the status of tenants to the mighty. Loyalty to Britain was their core self-identification and very lifeline, and what they came to fear from their leaders was loyalty's antithesis, betrayal.

Britain's decision in 1784 to turn the St. John River region into a colony called New Brunswick gave a hopeful appearance of new beginning. Yet it took only the calling of a provincial election to channel old grievances over insider dealing into renewed protests. Through electoral manipulation and criminal prosecutions the governing elite was able to defeat the alliance of self-made men who challenged them for power, but at what cost? Soon hundreds of Loyalist exiles affirmed their political troubles so great and their hopes for their new Loyalist colony so disappointed that they feared a new American revolution — in their midst.

The story of how these suspicions and troubles began back in British-occupied New York City, of how they turned into protests almost from the day the Loyalists landed at Saint John, and of how New Brunswick's governing elite finally silenced its critics through a startling campaign of political repression is the subject of this book. It shows how, at the very founding of Canada's Loyalist province, some exiled Loyalists clung to power by branding other Loyalist exiles with the high Loyalist crime of disloyalty.

NOTE ON
TERMINOLOGY

Loyal Americans trapped in the region of British-occupied
New York City at the end of the American Revolution
fell into two broad groups. The Refugees were civilian
Loyalists. Soldiers serving in one of the several dozen
military units raised in America to support the British
war effort were called Provincials. Most Refugee households evacuated from New York to St. John River came
as members of a militia company which, confusingly, had
no military function. Evacuees to what would become
the Maritime provinces were neither entitled to call
themselves, nor did they call themselves, United Empire
Loyalists, a distinction awarded to those who settled in the
old province of Quebec.

When Loyalist transport ships arrived at St. John harbour
in 1783 the area was part of Nova Scotia's Sunbury County.
It was not until June 18, 1784, that Britain included the
St. John River valley in a province called New Brunswick.
Separation from Nova Scotia became complete in November
with the public reading of the commission of newly arrived

Governor Thomas Carleton. By its constitutional documents New Brunswick was a British province, though more commonly it was called a colony. In 1867 New Brunswick became part of the federation called Canada.

Before 1783 the area at the mouth of the St. John River was called St. John (or St. John's) harbour. By year's end the two new Loyalist settlements on the harbour's east and west sides were designated Parr-town and Carleton respectively. In 1785 both were incorporated into a "city" called Saint John, although the older names remained in use. As a matter of convenience, this book makes free use of the term Saint John in the period prior to formal adoption of the name.

Quotations from eighteenth-century sources preserve their original spelling and capitalization. Superscripts have been lowered and punctuation has sometimes been standardized.

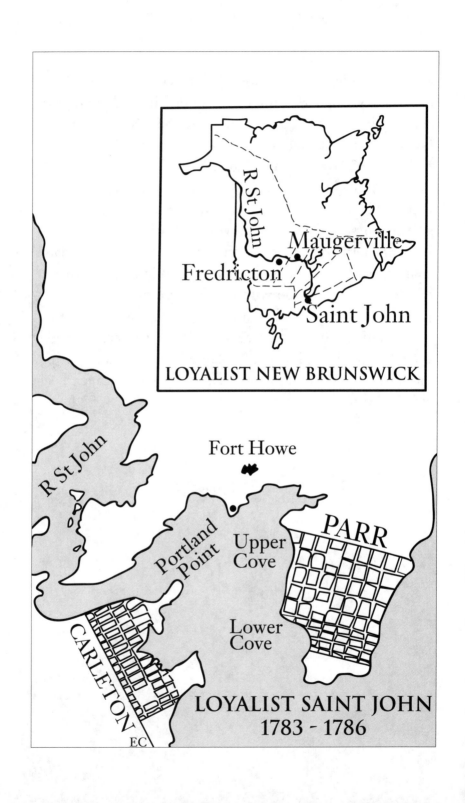

R St John

Fredricton

Maugerville

Saint John

LOYALIST NEW BRUNSWICK

R St John

Fort Howe

Portland Point

Upper Cove

PARR

Lower Cove

CARLETON

EC

LOYALIST SAINT JOHN
1783 - 1786

CHAPTER 1
OUR FATE SEEMS NOW DECREED

His crime against America was breaking the tea boycott.

Young Sylvanus Whitney was a small-time trader at Stamford, in the corner of Connecticut nearest New York City. In the spring of 1775 he began quiet dealing in the East India Company's fine Bohea tea. He took this risk even as most of his neighbours fell in with America's boycott of British tea to protest taxation of the colonies. Betrayed to Stamford's ominous Committee of Observation, Whitney was made to beg the "favour of the publick to overlook this my transgression." To drive the lesson home, local Patriots summoned fifes and drums and marched the tea in grand procession to a gallows. Here they ceremoniously hanged, then burnt it.[1]

With the usual three huzzas the mob dispersed, leaving the tea's owner to ponder the message of the ashes. He had been spared tar and feathers. In return, he had pledged to behave "as a true friend to my Country." But what country? At the close of the American crisis Sylvanus Whitney would lead a company of fellow Connecticut Loyalists on their voyage of exile to Nova Scotia's St. John River.

In the not very distant days of Whitney's childhood, America had been ardent in its attachment to king and empire, even if British policies caused occasional head-shaking. For the chronically disunited American colonies, Britain's army and navy were the only effective security against New France and its Amerindian allies. Whitney was a boy of nine in 1758 when the glorious news arrived that General Amherst had taken Louisbourg in Cape Breton, freeing New England from the French threat to the cod fishery. He was ten when word came through of Wolfe's cunning conquest of the mighty fortress of Quebec. With it, the French-Amerindian encirclement of Britain's continental colonies was finally smashed. How the bells rang out along the Atlantic seaboard. From the St. Lawrence valley down to the Gulf of Mexico, from the Mississippi eastward to the Atlantic, from Newfoundland to the Floridas: now all was *British*.

It was just a generation later that Britain was made to surrender the best bits of this vast empire. She gave them up not to France or Spain but to the very colonists whose safety had been won at such cost a generation earlier. Contemporaries marvelled at this world turned upside down. We share their wonder today. How surprising that Americans who had gloried in the national triumph over the French should rise up against those very bonds of nationhood. How much more surprising that their rebellion should succeed.

Despite its unlikely outcome the American crisis had deep roots. On paper Britain's colonial officials were nearly all-powerful. In practice the elected branch of colonial assemblies had come to see themselves as miniature versions of the House of Commons, especially in taxing, spending and accounting for public money. When the real Parliament in London imposed taxes on America, beginning in the mid-1760s, colonial politicians and intellectuals denounced it as oppressive and wrong. The power to tax, they claimed, was held by their local representatives alone. But to the British way of thinking, king and Parliament were supreme in all matters whatsoever. Each side saw the other as the aggressor. Stubbornly the British responded to colonial resistance with ever more coercive laws. As Massachusetts was at the forefront of tax resistance, it was to Boston that the army came in 1774 to overawe the province into submission. When daring local "Patriots," as they called themselves, ambushed a 1775 expedition to Lexington and Concord and then laid siege to Army-occupied Boston itself, colonists all down the Atlantic seaboard rose up in arms. Resistance had become rebellion.

As long as the American crisis was about the right to tax, colonists with an opinion were fairly united in opposing Parliament. But as the Patriots moved to take up arms, many of their neighbours drew back. When the intercolonial Congress declared independence for thirteen of the mainland colonies, thousands upon thousands of supporters of American rights became opponents of American separation. They saw more to fear from local hotheads and petty tyrants than a distant George III. Yet it's hard to generalize about those who kept loyal to the idea of empire even as their neighbours gambled on independence. In a crisis that lasted from the 1760s to the 1780s and disrupted political cultures all the way from Nova Scotia to Barbados, the line between Patriot and Loyalist shifted greatly by place and time.

At one extreme was New England. Here royal power collapsed even before the British army abandoned Boston in

1776. It's unsurprising, then, that few supporters of empire, apart from Anglican congregations in western Connecticut, ever dared make their private sentiments public. At the other extreme, the army's long occupation of the southern Hudson Valley of New York made that region — especially Manhattan, Staten and the adjacent part of Long islands — a citadel of colonial loyalism. As well as sheltering Loyalists whose home lay within its lines, the area became a magnet and asylum for thousands of loyal refugees fleeing Patriot-controlled areas. From the mass of Loyalists from all colonies crowded here in the lower Hudson Valley the future exiles to the St. John River in the Bay of Fundy would be drawn.

TO STAND BY HIS MAJESTY'S LAW AND GOVERNMENT

As America's political crisis descended into civil war, it parted friends and set neighbour against neighbour, sibling against sibling. Patriots in all thirteen rebelling colonies made repressive anti-Loyalist laws. Ten of the thirteen sent active Loyalists to the gallows. The banished, expelled, displaced and otherwise dispossessed numbered many tens of thousands. Yet not all Loyalists in Patriot-controlled areas were treated harshly. Coercion might be restrained.[2] If Loyalists repented and pledged allegiance to their new state Congress, nothing dire might happen. That was how the Patriots handled Sylvanus Whitney, whose bloodless humiliation became a lesson for the whole town. Even when arrested, Loyalists might be released on their own parole or by giving a bond for future good behaviour.

Loyalists regarded as stubborn or dangerous were gaoled or sent to internal exile. Many more were threatened, mobbed, beaten and dispossessed. George Harding, an Ulster County, New York farmer, was so active a Loyalist that he soon became "obnoxious" to his Patriot neighbours. Threatened, he made the life-changing decision to leave farm and family and slip down the Hudson to the safety of Staten Island. Another loyal New York farmer, Daniel Parent of Westchester, hesitated longer and paid a price. When he refused to take up arms with the Patriots, they confiscated his goods, threatened him with a cocked pistol at his breast, humiliated him before his family and "run him Six miles with horses across the fields, making him let down the fenses and whiping him with the Butt ends of their hors whips." Then they granted Parent a pass to enter Army lines, the "ixpress" words of which read, "Daniel Parent is to pass with three days provisions with two dam'd old horses and a dam'd old waggon without any tire to it."[3]

The experiences of two brothers in the part of Connecticut facing Long Island present further variations on the theme that led thousands of colonists to slip behind British lines. Lawyer Fyler Dibblee was a captain of the Stamford training band (militia). After the fighting at Lexington in neighbouring Massachusetts, he refused to lead his company to reinforce the Patriot siege of Boston. Instead, he helped intercept gunpowder intended for use against the army and got up a petition to "stand by his Majesty's law and Government." As local Patriots grew angry, Dibblee and other neighbourhood men escaped into New York. Rebels retaliated by turning his wife and five children out of their home. Destitute, they lived on the charity of Dibblee's elderly father, an Anglican missionary, until able to join Fyler on Long Island. Even here raiders from the mainland pillaged them repeatedly.

Then Stamford Patriots exiled Fyler's younger brother Frederick to a remote corner of the state. They allowed him back in 1777, but when they pressed him to resist a royalist raiding party, Frederick refused and made his escape across Long Island Sound to join his brother, leaving parents and sisters to much sad persecution.[4]

The pattern of events that drove Frederick Dibblee into army-occupied New York had countless parallels among those Americans who would end their days in exile. The kept their heads down in rebel territory until the arrival of loyal forces compelled them to declare their allegiance. If they refused to join the invaders, they were treated as enemies. If they refused to serve with the Patriots against royal raiders — as with Daniel Parent and Frederick Dibblee — or if they actually assisted the pro-government military, they faced retaliation once it withdrew. Snared in this dilemma, many took the fateful step of attaching themselves to the army, accompanying it when it moved on.

A classic instance involving many future exiles to the St. John River was British General William Tryon's incursion into Connecticut in the summer of 1779. It was then that Silas Raymond, a Norwalk carpenter, revealed his Loyalist sympathies and felt compelled to flee. On evacuation he set fire to his own house, vowing that Patriots should not have it.[5] Another evacuee during the same raid was John Sayre, Anglican missionary at Fairfield. Early in the troubles he had stopped leading public worship because of the prohibition on prayers for the king. This action, and his refusal to sign a Patriot pledge, marked him as an enemy of independence. His home was surrounded by more than two hundred armed horsemen, his name was pilloried in "every store, mill, mechanical shop and public house," and like Frederick Dibblee he was banished. In July 1779, with Tryon's temporary occupation of Fairfield, Sayre withdrew with the king's troops into occupied New York.[6]

Most Americans were never confronted with the crisis that changed the lives of Sayre, Raymond and the Dibblee brothers. The grand military developments of the war spared most in New England, and many in other regions, the dilemma of deciding whether to make their private sentiments public. In this way the great majority of loyal-leaning colonists survived to become citizens of the new republic in 1783. They were spared any thought of exile. But those who lived near the British headquarters region of southern New York were denied the luxury of being passive Loyalists. There were so many incursions like that of Tryon on both sides that thousands were forced to the dreadful crisis of allegiance that led them to flee for safety within British lines. So it was that most of the exiles who found refuge, first at New York and later in the Bay of Fundy region of Nova Scotia, were driven to that step not so much by political principle as by accident of geography and war. They left because they could not stay.[7]

A DAMNABLE SERIES OF TREATING AND RETREATING

The movement into New York City of Loyalists from the Stamfords, Norwalks and Fairfields, magnified a hundred times by evacuations from Philadelphia, Charleston and Savannah, added greatly to the population at the mouth of the Hudson. When General William Howe secured the area in the summer of 1776, about five thousand inhabitants remained. Half a year later the civilian population had more than doubled. By the time of the great evacuation fleets of 1783 it stood at 33,000, as well as about 35,000 troops and their dependants.[8]

For the farmers of Staten and Long islands this was the best of times. They strove to meet the army's staggering demand for hay and wood. But the refugees crowded within government lines, where food, fuel and shelter were dear and employment was scarce, lacked normal means of supporting themselves. They turned for help to government and the army. Many got rooms in abandoned Patriot houses. For a fortunate few hundred, there were cash allowances, calculated according to the recipient's station in life. Quarterly payments ranged from fifty pounds to the Massachusetts grandee George Leonard, to twenty-five pounds for the Pennsylvania printer Christopher Sower, to trivial sums awarded some of the women. Many others drew rations and fuel from the army's commissariat. Official charity was not confined to unsupported women. Anglican clerics and lawyers figured prominently, as did Sanford Oliver, soon to be the controversial sheriff of St. John County in the Bay of Fundy.

Hundreds of families found support by placing men in one of several dozen provincial regiments formed in the American provinces to assist the regular army. The raising of such a unit was usually entrusted to a great landowner, such as Oliver De Lancey of New York or James Chalmers of Maryland. Their own commissions became effective when they had enlisted a minimum number of troops. To accomplish this they promised officer standing to those who went out and actually signed up recruits. Thus,

George Harding brought in thirty men from the country and enlisted them in the Guides and Pioneers, for which he became a lieutenant. James Grant recruited so many that he was made a major in Edmund Fanning's King's American Regiment. The raising of such corps was a typical eighteenth-century speculation, offering rank and respectable employment for colonial aristocrats and a supply of patronage appointments for their relatives and connections. Although this sometimes put "Coxcombs — Fools — & Blackguards" into positions of authority, the system worked well at finding soldiers, especially early in the war when the British were niggardly with inducements to enlist. The thirteen rebelling colonies provided about twenty thousand soldiers for provincial units.[9]

Yet there never was a Loyalist army under the strategic command of Loyalist leaders in the same sense that the Patriot side had its Continental Army. At first, the British were confident of victory, so they saw no need to build a powerful Loyalist military. They used the Provincials to construct fortifications, man garrisons and guard prisoners. Only after the regular army's disaster at Saratoga in 1777 and the resulting parliamentary reluctance to continue the war did the Provincials become vital to the strategy for saving the continent. Given the opportunity to fight, some units served with distinction. Despite this elevation in status and an intensified recruitment effort, willingness to enlist fell off markedly in the latter years of war. With France entering on the side of the enemy in 1778, and the remarkable failure of British arms, there was good reason for prudent men to await the outcome of the conflict from the sidelines.[10]

At the opposite end of the Loyalist military spectrum

were the militia units on the New York islands that did much to secure the region against Patriot guerrilla raids. From 1780 onwards service was compulsory for males aged between sixteen and sixty. The city militia patrolled streets, did guard duty and the like. On rural Staten Island, a local militia colonel recalled, his men had charge of the advanced posts in view of the enemy on the New Jersey mainland.[11] Here they built redoubts, transported artillery and rounded up waggons, horses, forage, fuel and small boats to meet the insatiable demands of the regular army.

Another avenue of military service was signing up with one of a number of paramilitary bands, mostly under the umbrella of the Associated Loyalists. Though they never numbered more than a few hundred, these volunteers became notorious in revolutionary history and mythology for their destructive raids into rebel territory. Their aim was vengeance and plunder.[12] They would destroy or seize enemy supplies (especially cattle) and kidnap prominent Patriots for ransom or exchange. In local terms they were highly effective, especially in supplying occupied New York with livestock for slaughter. The intensity with which the Associates and their Patriot counterparts inflicted hardship, abduction and even torture on civilians led to enduring bitterness in the New York City area, making it seem impossible for Loyalists to stay behind at war's end.

As headquarters for the army in North America, New York City was a base for many hundreds of British and Loyalist military gentry. The city's press campaigned against boredom by promoting their theatricals, concerts, dinners, assemblies, lectures, hurley matches and charitable occasions. Many of the names were soon to become familiar at St.

John harbour. The Reverend Mr. Sayre, for example, having fled his Connecticut home, supplemented his missionary stipend by lecturing on the magic of electricity. Prominent among future Saint Johners to offer public amusement were the Brooklyn tavern-keepers Charles Loosley and Thomas Elms, whose *Pro Bono Publico* motto was everywhere in the press. With well-tuned organ, billiard tables and flair for showmanship, the financially feckless Loosely and his partner were two of New York's most colourful civilians. As well as fortnightly subscription assemblies, they sponsored cricket matches and horse races and supplied foxes for hunting and bulls for baiting.[13]

Despite such distractions, the morale of Loyalists at New York was rarely high. Economically, they were insecure against the inflated price of most necessities. Politically, though suffering for their loyalty to the constitution, they lived under a military dictatorship. The lower Hudson region was secure enough to revert to civilian control, but the British allowed the governor and mayor to exercise no formal civil power and the chief justice held no court. As the war dragged on and a clear win became unlikely, the hardships of life in an armed camp made even ardent Loyalists grow sullen.

Their misery was compounded by the conduct of the British and German soldiers and sailors stationed among them. Colonial civil wars were a novelty and soldiers hardly knew how to behave towards civilians. Consider the experience of some New England exiles on Long Island, future migrants to the Bay of Fundy. They were plundered by British sailors, supposedly in the neighbourhood to protect them. On their protesting this treatment, the British captain threatened to "blow them to Hell if they came alongside [his ship] again, telling them he would give them no redress nor protection, but he would have his revenge before he left the station."[14]

Loyalist morale was corroded even more by the notion — which hardened into certainty by the beginning of the 1780s — that British military commanders had turned what looked like inevitable victory into catastrophic humiliation. Early in the occupation of New York, when there was an immediate opportunity to shatter Washington's untried Continental Army, the British chose the high road of conciliation. Eventually Loyalists came to despise this as characteristic dithering. If only *they* had been allowed to run the war! One keen observer of war policy was the muster master of provincial forces, Edward Winslow. By 1778 Winslow was condemning British strategy as "a damnable series of treating & retreating — Pidling, Conciliating & Commissioning." After two years of further slippage, Winslow still hoped to see a general "that's neither a Rebel or a Histerical Fool at the Head of a British Army in America & when that happens I shall have no doubt that the war will terminate as every true friend to the constitution wishes."[15]

But soon the "true friends" of a united empire were to have their final, crushing military disappointment with the surrender of Cornwallis at Yorktown in 1781, effectively ending the land war. And the British were to deal the Loyalists one still heavier blow. They had lost the war. Now they would lose the peace negotiations.

OUR FATE SEEMS NOW DECREED

With the humiliation at Yorktown, large-scale military activity on the American mainland ceased. The Loyalist community at New York and even the new commander-in-chief, Guy Carleton, hoped that a military solution was still possible, as the Patriots were divided and nearly bankrupt. But British public opinion was demanding an end to the sad spectacle and a government took office that was set on making peace with the colonies in order to concentrate on war with France and Spain. As much as anything on the battlefield, it was the flawed peace provisions that led to the flight of tens of thousands of Loyalists trapped at New York to the Bay of Fundy region.

After Yorktown most Loyalists knew that peace talks would follow, but few imagined that Britain would grant *independence* to the united colonies, at least not to all of them. Neither the military position nor the sentiments of the inhabitants would justify giving up southern New York. Snared as they now were in the former refuge of loyalty at the mouth of the Hudson, they remained hopeful. Nothing prepared them for the news reaching New York in the summer of 1782 that London had opened peace negotiations by conceding independence to all thirteen colonies in rebellion. Independence had not even been a bargaining point. Strategically the move seemed incredible. Practically it meant that Britain's chances of wresting solid guarantees for the person and property of Loyalists in an independent America were infinitely weaker. It announced that Britain's peace strategy had completed their ruin.

To grasp the poignancy of the dilemma that unfolded in the evacuations a year later, it is necessary to understand that at this point — mid 1782 — the impulse of most of those trapped at New York City was to make their own peace with the new order. Though loyal to empire, they were Americans. The British government, far from regretting a general Loyalist reconciliation to the new republic, simply assumed that it would happen. Thousands, both Refugees and Provincials, did try to slip into rebel territory, hoping to conceal their past. But the Patriots would not be reconciled. After independence became certain, there was a move in the embittered countryside around New York City to drive the remaining known Loyalists into government lines. Westchester County was the scene of great violence. War-ravaged New Jersey continued to send Loyalists to the gallows. And Patriot war parties did not stop their raids.

Those Loyalists who, under the provisional peace terms, returned into Patriot-held territory to inspect what remained of their property or visit family were beaten, robbed and expelled. When Solomon Ferris, an evacuee to the St. John River in the June 1783 fleet, revisited his native Greenwich to collect his family, Patriots seized him for his role in a raid on that place in 1779, after which he and two other future Saint John evacuees had been sentenced to death. Now, at his bail hearing, he claimed the protection of the articles of peace but was answered that Connecticut's policy was to prosecute Loyalists. Similarly, when sixty-two-year-old William Foshay returned up the Hudson to his home at Philipsburgh, New York after eighteen months within government lines, the local Patriot commissar ordered the sickly old man expelled, shaking his sword over Foshey's head and telling him to get his "corpse" to Nova Scotia.

Foshay's grey hairs had not spared him, and neither did John Segee's youth. The son of a soldier in the Loyal American Regiment, this teenager with one arm crossed to the mainland to visit friends. Patriots caught and whipped him, shaved his head, threatened to behead him, and sent him back to let his friends on Long Island know "that every Rascal of them that attempted to come among them would meet with the like treatment."[16] It was this continuing rebel persecution, well publicized in the press, that convinced tens of thousands to take the life-transforming decision to leave New York ahead of the army, no matter what a peace agreement might say.

The final text of the treaty in which Solomon Ferris had put his trust in vain confirmed that there was no future in the new republic for Loyalists stranded at New York. With groans and hisses they greeted news arriving in March 1783 that the British had won not even a paper guarantee that they might continue to live unpersecuted in their homeland. The Patriot Congress would merely "earnestly recommend" to state governments that laws confiscating the property of civilian Loyalists be "reconsidered." Even less protection was held out to Provincials. And so the only course for tens of thousands in the once asylum — now trap — of New York City became exile.

Anger at the British government's betrayal was exceeded only by despair. "The people's consternation on this news is not in the power of the ablest pen to describe," wrote one Loyalist. What would become of them? "It is impossible," said a British observer, "to describe the Melancholly Effect the News had upon Thousands of Loyalists, & Refugees, who are oblig'd to abandon their Country, & seek Assylum in Nova-Scotia." Stranded at New York, the Massachusetts refugee Sally Winslow voiced a despair that filled many hearts:

"[O]ur fate seems now decreed, and we are left to mourn out our days in wretchedness. Know other recourse for millions, but to submit to the tyranny of exulting enemys or settle a new country...The open enemys of Great Britain have gained their point and more than ever they could have had impudence to have asked for — while their brave, persevereing Noble Friends, who have suffer'd and toil'd for years...are left without friends, without fortune, without prospect of support...This Peace brings none to my heart."[17]

So it was that heartsick, panicking Loyalists trapped at New York, ruined in war by British generals, ruined in peace by politicians and still persecuted by vengeful Patriots and their state governments, were forced to contemplate the bitter fate of exile. Because Patriot zeal against them actually intensified in 1783, even as the evacuation from New York was underway, the final number who scrambled onto ships far exceeded the authorities' expectations. Defending his long delay in surrendering the city to General Washington, Guy Carleton, the British commander, complained that almost all people within British lines were convinced their very lives depended on leaving before the victors took possession.[18]

The forced evacuation of New York City was one of the great co-ordinated population movements of the eighteenth century. More than a year elapsed between the first evacuation flotilla, in October 1782, and the final organized departures. To the wealthy or well-connected, Britain remained the refuge of choice, at least for a time. Upwards of five thousand Loyalists were in Britain by war's end. For the adventuresome, resettlement in Quebec was one possibility, the West Indian islands another. But to most of those trapped in the former asylum of loyalty at the mouth of the Hudson, the most realistic avenue of escape was to Nova Scotia. Although that northern outpost of New England had never had a favourable reputation in the older colonies, it was within a week's sail of New York in the right vessel and was known to be habitable. As its population was small, likely there would be large tracts of vacant land in good situations. By the time Carleton finally surrendered the city to Washington's Continentals in November 1783, the army had sent upwards of thirty thousand loyal migrants to Nova Scotia alone.

The scale of official British charity towards the American exiles had no precedent.[19] It recognized that the Loyalists had made themselves targets by responding to repeated appeals from government and could not now be left to martyrdom. Grants of land, provisions during the resettlement process, pensions for life to officers of disbanded provincial regiments, and financial compensation for loss of property, office and professional income were among the many "bounties" for the displaced.

This generosity was unplanned. Grant of a half-pay pension to Provincial officers was spurred by a parliamentary resolution that ran completely contrary to long-stated government policy. The British offer to transport willing Loyalists into exile was made almost casually in early 1782, when government had no idea that Patriot persecutions would make escape seem necessary to a large number. When that reality unfolded in 1783, London was too remote to shape events. It was Guy Carleton on the spot at New York who crafted government's easy promises from the previous year into undertakings that would run years into the future, and even Carleton and his staff marvelled at the scale of the exodus. The impetus to compensate Loyalists financially arose from the American failure to live up to the peace treaty, a possibility the British had thought remote. On the whole,

Britain merely stumbled into a pattern of commitment to the loyal exiles that would prove decisive to the future political character of a continent.

Arrangements on behalf of New York–area Loyalists considering evacuation northward were made by voluntary "associations" in negotiation with the commander-in-chief and with the governor of Nova Scotia. There were many such associations. The Westchester Refugees, one of the Loyalist paramilitary units, chose to settle the Fort Cumberland region at the head of the Bay of Fundy, familiar to many colonials from service there during the Seven Years' War. Another group, made up of Baptist and Quaker refugees, made its way to New Brunswick's future Charlotte County. Fifty-five boldly pretentious Loyalists formed their own resettlement group; as we will see, this particular manoeuvre would resonate in Loyalist politics for years to come. Most officers and men in the provincial corps formed an association of their own. Free blacks, too, organized themselves for exile. The great majority of white civilians joined either the Port Roseway Associates, proposing to settle the harbour in peninsular Nova Scotia that became known as Shelburne, or the Bay of Fundy Adventurers, proposing to settle the St. John River and the neighbourhood of Annapolis Royal.

OFF AT LAST!

In mid-1782 the earliest group of "Refugees" (as civilian Loyalists were called, to distinguish them from "Provincials" or military Loyalists) to join the Bay of Fundy Adventurers chose a board of agents. This "New York Agency" drew up a list of assistance needed for resettlement and presented it to the army's commander-in-chief. Among the requests were transport to Nova Scotia, provisions for one year, clothing, medicines, building materials, farming utensils, mill equipment and weapons. All of this Guy Carleton was willing to grant. But in response to the agency's central request for 300 to 600 acres of surveyed land for each family he could only recommend their petition to Nova Scotia's governor, John Parr. Still, Carleton's response had been warmly supportive. With this assurance the Bay of Fundy Adventurers began an active campaign for members.

The first Bay of Fundy Adventurers left New York for Nova Scotia almost immediately, in the autumn of 1782. Because the agency had not yet sent explorers to spy out locations for new settlements, this party sailed to the village of Annapolis Royal. Numbering about 460 people, it arrived in a convoy off Nova Scotia's old capital on October 19, 1782, along with three representatives of the New York Agency. Their mission was to explore the colony for settlement sites and to secure assistance from Governor Parr's administration at Halifax. Their November tour up the St. John River produced an enthusiastic report. The St. John waterway, they gushed, was equal to the Connecticut or the Hudson and navigable by ships for 80 miles inland. The lush intervale land of the Maugerville area in the central river valley produced crops of all kinds with little labour: perfect vegetables, parsnips of fantastic length, and so on.[20] This rich description delighted the agents back at New York, who rushed it into the press.

Because evacuation of New York's civilians was a co-operative effort between the various individual Loyalist associations and the army, Refugees intending to sail northward at public expense had to both join an organization such as the Bay of Fundy Adventurers and to register with the military bureaucracy. Without a special pass no one could leave at government expense who had not lived a year behind army lines.[21] Suddenly, on April 16, when many were already aboard ship, Carleton ordered that an official committee adjust the debts of evacuees. Intended to protect creditors amid a mass exodus of debtors, this new rule plunged scores of intending evacuees into financial despair. One of them was Elizabeth Lester, whose husband had already gone to the St. John River in the May fleet. In order to sail northward herself she had to appeal to Carleton for help to pay debts contracted in caring for four sick children.[22] There were scores of such pleas: from Joshua Gidney, wife and nine children ("Large and Almost Naked family"); from Jacob Holder ("his necessity great"); from Jacob Hart and wife (aged seventy five and "ready to imbark for Nova Scotia without a Shilling to Support him"); from Conrad Gunter ("destitute of Money and other Necessarys of Life"); from Dianna Bush Willcocks ("no longer able to suport herself & Children"); from Jotham Hawxhurst, wife and four children ("Reduced to such Extreme poverty that himself and family must Unavoidably suffer"); from Robert Thorn, Jacob Brill, Caleb Powell and families ("really in Distress'd Condition"); from Northrup Marple, wife and six children ("truly distressed for the want of every necessary of Life"). Anglican clerics John and James Sayre and several others appealed to the public for donations to assist emigrants in similarly desperate circumstances. Evacuation ship passenger lists designated some families as objects of charity, perhaps making them eligible for extra rations.

Widows Rachel Ogden and Sarah Wheeler, travelling northward in June, had a more ambitious plea for Carleton:

could each be allowed to take to the St. John River a pair of "servants"? Probably these servants were black, although not necessarily slaves.[23] In the evacuation of New York, black civilians, of whatever status, were subject to a special control. If free, many had won that status by responding to British invitations to desert rebel owners, some of whom then tried to reclaim them at war's end. Carleton refused to surrender blacks who had achieved freedom in this manner but he did promise General Washington to prevent any other escaped slaves from fleeing to Nova Scotia. For this purpose a committee, including representatives of the Congress, examined three thousand embarking civilian blacks.[24] They told many stories. Francis Griffin, a forty-five-year-old "stout fellow," scrambled on board the *Clinton* bound for the Bay of Fundy only after having been kidnapped by agents of his alleged owner. While Griffin was preparing for a new life in Nova Scotia his abductors were sentenced to fines and the stocks for their crime. A subtler drama played out when James Peters arrived back from the St. John River to arrange to ship his servants northward. Among them was twenty-year-old Cairo. Pompey, Cairo's freeborn husband, was a servant of the commander-in-chief himself. It fell to Peters to appeal to Carleton to release Pompey so that he could join Cairo on the voyage.[25]

A different sort of appeal came from a lieutenant in the North Carolina Volunteers. At the end of April, Thomas Coffield had wed Martha Carman on Long Island. When time came for Coffield and bride to take ship for the St. John River, Martha's anxious mother kept her hidden, leaving Coffield to publish a humiliating caution to merchants against giving his new wife goods on credit.[26]

How much property could departing Loyalists carry on public transports? Shipping was in short supply, and the proliferation of auction notices in the New York newspapers for 1783 suggests that the British would not allow the exiles to ship much in the way of household goods at public expense.[27] This would help explain why about one in ten civilian Loyalists going to the St. John River hired passage on private ships, taking with them the pigs, cattle, nails, glass, hinges, carpentry tools and lumber needed to start life anew in a wilderness.

Six fleets of transport ships carried at least ten thousand loyal exiles from New York to the mouth of the St. John River in 1783 at public expense. Five comprised mostly civilian Refugees in the Bay of Fundy Adventurers. A sixth fleet carried disbanding Provincials and their families. A few of the ships used for transport belonged to the Navy, but most were hired contractors. If the state of the ill-fated *Martha* (rotten sails, undermanned) is an indication, the military were not over-scrupulous in what captains and ships they engaged.

FIRST (MAY, OR "SPRING") FLEET

The May fleet of the Bay of Fundy Adventurers to the future Saint John was more fully under the direction of the New York Agency than the army would later allow. Having decided by February 1783 to focus efforts on the St. John River, the agency began preparations to send a fleet northward as soon as weather permitted. Most other evacuation associations had the same idea. To promote the little-known St. John region, and perhaps in a spirit of rivalry with the Port Roseway Associates, the agency publicized its venture in the press and by personal lobbying. One traveller with the May fleet recalled that John

Sayre combined his priestly office with boosterism so effectively that he enrolled most of his congregation at Eaton's
Neck, future settlers of Kingston, Kings County.[28]

Embarkation of thousands of Refugee families, many
with small children, and their baggage from all parts of
the British-controlled New York region, and destined for
four separate points in Nova Scotia, proved an enormous
undertaking. The loading process began as early as April 1
and took three weeks. With some ships bound for Halifax
and Annapolis Royal, and many for Shelburne and St. John
harbour, there was congestion and confusion as evacuees for
each port were collected at several loading points. The New
York Agency's attempt at internal co-ordination consisted
only of sending one of its number, James Peters, along with
the fleet and in designating a leading Refugee on each transport ship as a sort of deputy agent. Lawyer Fyler Dibblee
styled himself as "appointed to have the Care of the People
in the Union." Similarly, Solomon Willard was superintend-
ent of Refugees on board the *Ariel*.[29] It's likely that groups of
old or new friends, drawn together at New York in common
misfortune, arranged to take passage in the same vessel.

Nearly fifty sail, including private vessels, left Sandy
Hook, New Jersey, for Nova Scotia on Sunday, April 27,
in a fleet commodored by Henry Mowat. Eighteen transports of civilian Refugees were destined for Shelburne, one
for Annapolis Royal and ten for the St. John River (*Ariel*,
Aurora, *Brothers*, *Camel*, *Grand Duchess of Russia*, *Hope*, *Mars*,
Sovereign, *Spencer*, *Union*). Also destined for Saint John were
a number of Provincials and their dependants in the *Lady's
Adventure*, mostly of the King's American Dragoons. Other
vessels brought baggage, provisions and horses. On the

fourth day out, the fleet was scattered off the Nantucket shoals, so that when the *Union* sailed into St. John harbour on May 10 it was alone.[30] Two days later most ships had caught up and the Loyalists were preparing anxiously for their first encounter with the inhospitable landscape. Arriving civilians numbered about 1,700. Military arrivals were about 325 men, 75 dependants and 40 "servants."

SECOND (JUNE) FLEET

As the May fleet sailed from New York, preparations for the next group exodus to Nova Scotia began. To simplify control over this and future embarkations, the agency decided that now all Bay of Fundy Adventurers would be divided into companies. Companies were intended to have 125 people but some had several times that number while others proved much smaller. Each would elect a captain, who appointed two lieutenants. All three would receive commissions from the commander-in-chief as militia officers. (The text and charts that follow refer to these various companies by their captains' names.) This mode of organization was a convenience in embarking large numbers of Refugees and in issuing and accounting for the many forms of royal bounty. Equally, the company system provided Refugees with an elected leadership that would continue to be recognized in Nova Scotia. These so-called "militia" companies, which had no militia function, were both a means of hierarchical control and a potential forum for voicing grievances. So it would prove.

   This second 1783 fleet was supposed to leave New York at the end of May. The journal of Sarah Scofield Frost, who with her shoemaker husband and two children sailed in the militia company of Sylvanus Whitney (the ex-tea trader), records that she and some two hundred other Refugees boarded the *Two Sisters* for Nova Scotia on Sunday, May 25. There they remained for three tedious weeks while other vessels were readied. Not until June 7 did the agency give notice that it was absolutely necessary for members of the various companies to board by the following evening, and even this was a false alarm. Frost relieved her frustration at the continued delay with teas, card playing, buying expeditions on shore, berry picking and visiting friends. Overcrowding on the ship (there were seven families in the Frost cabin), confusion, howling infants, heat and nausea from riding at anchor were a slow torture: "Our people seem cross and quarrelsome," she complained. Only on June 16 could she exclaim that they were "Off at last!"[31] Even then the voyage northward, slowed by calm air and days of impenetrable fog, took more than two weeks.

The largest part of this June fleet consisted of fifteen militia companies on ten transports bound for St. John harbour. Another company of Bay of Fundy Adventurers went to Annapolis Royal. The fleet also included one company of the Port Roseway Associates and several hundred of the paramilitary Westchester Loyalists bound for the Cumberland region. By now the British were scrounging for transport capacity. *Amity's Production*, for example, was a mast ship pressed into service. Soon after the fleet's departure, a few smaller vessels started for Saint John with officers seconded from provincial units. They were ordered northward to handle small river craft intended for local transport of surveyors, provisions and settlers. On July 5 the main fleet, carrying about 1,200 Refugees, made its general landing at St. John harbour.

Transport	Unit Captain
Amity's Production	Thomas Welsh
Bridgewater	Joseph Clark, James Hayt, Christopher Benson, Joseph Forrester
Duchess of Gordon	Asher Dunham, Abiathar Camp
Generous Friends	Thomas Elms
Hopewell	Henry Thomas
Littledale	Peter Berton
Symmetry	John Forrester
Tartar	Oliver Bourdett
Thames	John Cock
Two Sisters	Sylvanus Whitney, Joseph Gorham

THIRD (JULY) FLEET

A third influx of about one thousand Loyalists from New York to St. John harbour boarded ship at the end of June, departing about July 8. This July fleet was smaller, but it resembled the June exodus in that almost all passengers were bound for Saint John rather than Annapolis or

Shelburne. The first ship to reach port, the *Ann*, arrived by July 24.

Transport	Unit Captain
Ann	Robert Chillas
Aurora	William Perrine, John Oblenis
Commerce	Peter Huggeford, Peter Berton
Elizabeth	Richard Hill, Nathaniel Horton, William Olive
Grace	Thomas Welsh, Richard Squires, Daniel Fowler
Joseph	Donald Drummond
Lord Townsend	John Mersereau, Jacob Cook
Montague	Peter Huggeford
Sovereign	John Menzies
Three Sisters	Thomas Huggeford, William Olive
William	William Wright

FOURTH (AUGUST) FLEET
The fourth of the monthly fleets from New York to the St. John River set sail about August 4, the first ship

arriving in port ten days later. Among more than six hundred passengers was John Sayre, de facto head of the Bay of Fundy Adventurers' New York Agency. The *Clinton* arrived somewhat later, on August 30. Its passengers were four companies of Free Black Refugees. Two days later it discharged sixty-one men, forty-one women and thirty children before carrying others over to Annapolis Royal.[32] At least two adults and perhaps as many as four children among those bound for Saint John had died during the short voyage from New York. With the *Clinton* arrivals came the dreaded smallpox.[33]

Transport	Unit Captain
Clinton	Free Blacks
Fishburn	William Grey
Grand Duchess of Russia	Nathaniel Chandler
Hesperus	?
Mary	John Cluett
Peggy	Joseph Cooper, William Walker
Sally	Peter Grim, Robert Campbell
Spencer	Peter Grim

FIFTH (SEPTEMBER OR "FALL") FLEET

When it became clear, late in 1782, that many Loyalists in and around New York City would not be permitted to reconcile with the victorious Patriots, the provincial military, like the civilian Refugees, formed an organization to find land in Nova Scotia. One of their agents for that purpose, Edward Winslow, sailed to Annapolis with the May 1783 fleet and later inspected the St. John River valley. The agents seem to have accomplished little, however, perhaps because the Provincials' fate depended on the attitude of their superiors in the British military. Although Guy Carleton foresaw a large exodus of Provincials to Nova Scotia as early as April 1783, it was mid-August before he gave them permission to leave, and it was September 27 before they reached St. John harbour, landing three days later. This was too late in the season to get to their promised land, even had detailed surveys been made, or to erect substantial shelters against the approaching winter. The Provincials may have been kept at New York for so long to safeguard its security and internal order. But it is more likely that Carleton delayed their evacuation because, with a shortage of transport, he thought it better to give priority to the less manageable civilians.

Transport	Unit
Ann	Guides and Pioneers, Loyal American Regiment
Apollo	King's American Dragoons, Loyal American Regiment
Camel	Baptists, Quakers
Commerce	3rd New Jersey Volunteers, 1st Pennsylvania Loyalists
Cyrus	James Dickinson, Nathaniel Merritt
Duke of Richmond	1st & 2nd New Jersey Volunteers
Eagle	John Smith
Elizabeth	American Legion; 3rd New Jersey Volunteers, Prince of Wales American Regiment
Esther	3rd New Jersey Volunteers
King George	King's American Regiment; Royal Garrison Battalion

Martha	Maryland Loyalists; 2nd De Lancey's
Montague	Prince of Wales American Regiment
Pallisar	2nd De Lancey's
Ranger	3rd New Jersey Volunteers
Sovereign	1st De Lancey's
William	King's American Regiment
It is uncertain what vessel carried the Queen's Rangers and a further part of the Prince of Wales American Regiment.	

Arrivals numbered more than three thousand men and dependants. In addition, a substantial portion of two provincial units was on the St. John River already. A detachment of Royal Fencible Americans had garrisoned Fort Howe for several years, and most of the King's American Dragoons had arrived at Saint John in May. These other units numbered nearly six hundred soldiers and dependants.

The worst accident of the entire Bay of Fundy migration occurred to the *Martha* of this fleet, carrying families of the Maryland Loyalists and 2nd De Lancey's. Old and undermanned, the vessel sank off Seal Island in the Bay of Fundy. The incompetent captain who ran the ship onto rocks was one of the first off, leaving the passengers to their fate. Ninety-nine lives were lost, but seventy-five were saved, carried by fishermen to St. John harbour. The most remarkable survivor was Elizabeth Beard Woodward, wife of a soldier in the Maryland Loyalists. When the ship struck and began breaking up she was great with child, or rather with triplets. In her own words, "she suffered unparalleled hardships, being pregnant, and with a child in her arms, remained three days on the wreck, was taken up with her husband and child by fishermen, off Marble Head, and shortly after being landed, delivered of three sons."34

A small number of civilian Refugees also sailed from New York to Saint John in September. The Royal Navy's *Camel* brought companies of Baptists, Quakers and a few others, totalling 260, into Saint John harbour in mid-month. Only two of the religious and three other Refugees disembarked; the rest took on three months' provisions and sailed on to Beaver Harbour.35 With the *Camel* came the *Cyrus* and the *Eagle* (also Royal Navy ships), which together carried more than four hundred Refugees.

SIXTH (OCTOBER) FLEET

The final organized evacuation fleet from New York reached St. John harbour about October 17. Eight ships carried 1,100 Refugees, though one, the *Nancy*, was delayed en route by the loss of masts and rigging and did not reach port until December. On board ship with the Refugees were perhaps 450 British and a few German regular soldiers. They were accepting the British invitation to settle in Nova Scotia. Loyalists had long since come to fear and despise the conduct of army soldiers. Unsurprisingly, the journal of one of the *Jason*'s crew records soldiers of the 42nd Regiment stealing from the members of Thomas Spragg's Refugee company and tossing pet dogs overboard.[36]

Ship	Unit/Captain
Alexander	Bartholomew Crannell
Jason	Thomas Spragg, 42nd Regiment
John & Jane	Robert Campbell, James Thorne, 7th, 17th, 37th and 38th regiments
Mary	John Ford
Mercury	Samuel Dickinson, 42nd Regiment
Nancy	Thomas Wooley, 38th and 40th Regiments
Neptune	Thomas Fairchild, Joseph Ferris, William Lewis, 40th Regiment
Sally	John Wetmore

FURTHER ARRIVALS

British forces quit New York City officially on November 25. The October fleet was the last large-scale evacuation to the St. John River, but small groups of Loyalists were still arriving into the following year. On December 14 the *Camel* was back at Saint John with latecomers. Thirteen were landed on that date; the others were allowed to remain on board throughout the winter. It was not until early March 1784 that the *Camel* left another thirty-one passengers at Saint John and the remaining sixty-eight at various points in Passamaquoddy. Among other late arrivals were thirteen attached to John Wetmore's Refugee company. By January 26 some of these had made it as far as Campobello, where they remained on this outpost of British government until they could move on to Saint John in the spring. Another late arrival was a party of sixteen regulars and dependants connected with the 42nd Regiment, sent from Halifax. It was also at this time that 183 of the King's Orange Rangers arrived at Quaco, a harbour east of the St. John River. In the spring of 1784 a further 124 civilian arrivals appeared on victualling records.

FEW PEOPLE OF ANY CONSEQUENCE HAVE LEFT US

The same transport ships that brought Loyalists to Saint John at public expense were free to accept paying passengers for the voyage back to New York. We can assume that many people took passage southward, either temporarily or because Patriot persecution now seemed preferable to the rocks and confusion found at this edge of the Nova Scotia wilderness. At the end of October the commissary of Fort Howe recorded nine heads of household just then sailing back. They gave varied reasons:

Benjamin Robson, 6 in family, all except one son
going on pretense of purchasing small vessels, to
return again soon.

James Morrel returning for his family, leaves two
servants.

Nicholas Howell returning for his family; has
built a small house.

Robert Tongate and wife returning as they say
to collect small debts, but the truth is he is turned
out of the society for stealing from some persons
in Captain Elm's company; he belongs to that
company.

Richard Penny, ten in family, returns because he
cannot support his family through the winter, has
drawn no provisions, says he has a house building
in the town at St. Johns.

Benjamin Haywood returns on account of getting
no employ — intends to come back in the spring.

Theodorick Bland, for trade.

Cap't [George] Bennison, for trade — has a good
character.

Miss Katy Hawser, returns (as she says) for a
husband.

Thomas Knox, who did a general re-muster of Loyalists in
1784, thought that already many had left the colony, having
run through their bounty of rations.[37]

There is no sure way of knowing how many returned to
the old colonies in the 1780s. Town histories in New York,
Connecticut and New Jersey show Loyalists reappearing
from Nova Scotia without incident, but the return is the least

studied aspect of the Loyalist diaspora. To the Saint John press as late as 1788 the continuing exodus of the discouraged was a "pregnant" evil. This is how a more optimistic merchant explained it to an English correspondent:

"The report you mention of all the Refugees going back as fast as they get [Loyalist Claim] compensation is groundless and false. Many its true have gone back to the States, some from one cause, some from another; but generally speaking those that have gone back were a set of poor wretches that had they staid here must have been supported by the publick at least every winter. Very few people of any consequence have left us."[38]

Perhaps these remarks are too defensive to carry complete conviction. Yet the very obscurity of the "poor wretches" who slipped back into the new republic as anti-Loyalist hostility abated means we will never have more than general impressions of the return exodus from the St. John valley in the 1780s.

CHAPTER 2
THE ROUGHEST LAND I EVER SAW

Sarah Scofield Frost's foggy, tedious, anxious voyage from New York ended when she awoke on June 28 to find the *Two Sisters* gliding quietly "nigh to land on both sides." Soon a local pilot came aboard. By noon the ship was anchored beneath the Fort Howe hill in St. John harbour. Some men went anxiously ashore "to see how it looks." When husband Billy brought back salmon and a specimen of wild pea blossoms Sarah resolved to get on shore herself. Defying the strutting Sylvanus Whitney, captain of their Refugee company, who thought women should keep out of the way, she declared that she would get ashore even if Billy must carry her — eight months pregnant — on his back.

After that day on land with Billy and the children, Sarah returned to the *Two Sisters* stunned by her encounter with the wind-stunted conifers and limestone terrain that was to become their Loyalist "city." Her usually chatty journal records numbly, "It is I think the roughest land I ever saw."[1]

Bleak though the prospect was to vulnerable exiles arriving from the green and pleasant land of southern New

York, the area around the mouth of the St. John River was sparsely settled already. Britain had claimed this western half of Nova Scotia since 1713, but its situation on the fault line between contesting French and British empires had kept away English-speaking settlers for decades. There was also the worry that the St. John Valley was the territory of the Malecites, the last entirely undisplaced tribe on the Atlantic seaboard. Only with the construction of Fort Frederick on the western side of St. John harbour in 1758 was there a British presence. With this encouragement, a Massachusetts partnership that included James Simonds, William Hazen and James White began a cluster of commercial activities at Portland Point on St. John harbour late in the 1760s. In 1778 the army replaced the abandoned Fort Frederick with Fort Howe, which protected against marauding Patriot privateers from New England and gave a further boost to local trading. Including Gilfred Studholme, the Fort Howe commandant, and his garrison of 118 Royal Fencible Americans and their dependants, there were about four hundred people at the river's mouth in 1783 to greet the first New York fleet.

I HAVE HITHERTO ACTED IN THE DARKE

In one way the political story of early Saint John echoes the very concern that wrecked Britain's American empire: was the authority of the settlement's decision-makers legitimate? The Loyalists had landed within the county of Sunbury and colony of Nova Scotia, where the machinery of local rule was suited to the needs of a scattered population numbering only a few hundred. It would hardly do for a concentration of thousands of despairing, unemployed exiles, many just set free from military discipline. How were Saint John Loyalists to be managed, and by what authority?

When the Bay of Fundy Adventurers, as the civilian Refugees were called, boarded public transports bound for Saint John, they remained under the direction of their New York Agency. First the army bureaucracy and then the government of Nova Scotia found this convenient. There was no other way to handle such a swarm of arrivals. Later, when the Provincial troops arrived on the scene and were disbanded, the Nova Scotia government regarded their chief officers as if they, too, continued to have authority over the men. In this way the agents and their provincial counterparts took on a key role in directing Saint John affairs during 1783 and much of 1784, the period when the town's political troubles had their origin. Whether the Refugees themselves expected to continue as wards of their agents is not clear. The agents themselves expected it, and it was a role to which they were naively unequal.

Had John Parr and his officers of colonial government at Halifax been prepared to receive and settle the Refugees and Provincials, matters might have gone very differently. Instead, the governor's handling of the settlement crisis was marked by timidity, lost opportunity and — as he saw it — lack of his own authority. At nearly every turn his officials were kept on a short leash by Parr's anxiety to have new instructions from far-off London, even as the loyal exiles were arriving by the thousand. In October 1782 Parr had written for clear direction on new land-granting in the largely empty colony.[2] Eight months later, with the May and June fleets already at St. John harbour, the requested author-ization had still not come. Defensively, he explained that

"Government has not yet honored me with their commands, relative to this vast Emigration; I have hitherto acted in the darke."[3] Not until September 1783, eleven months after the request, did the instructions arrive.

Parr's new orders made great concessions to the Loyalists. But even with these directives on land-granting — which arrived so late that it was not until the spring of 1784 at the earliest that the Loyalists were able to get to their land — Parr's administration was hampered by practical difficulties. No one had a clear idea how many Refugees and Provincials were coming to Nova Scotia or just where they were going. In the case of the St. John River, both Refugees and Provincials laid claim to the more desirable lower tracts of the river valley. Surveyor-General Charles Morris expressed Halifax's perplexity at finding that two different sets of people had chosen the same place for a settlement without first advising each other or the colony's government.[4] He predicted "ill will and great confusion." He was right.

Despite the lack of timely direction from London, the unprecedented nature of the task, the clamorous and disorganized state of the immigrants and the logistical stumbling blocks, the Halifax administration did attempt a good deal, even during those many months when the governor was "in the darke." Within three weeks of his own arrival in the colony in the fall of 1782, Parr launched the process for escheating (cancelling) wilderness township land grants with a view to settling arrivals expected the following spring. For the St. John River the Halifax administration initiated land surveys as soon as the first fleet arrived. On May 7 the surveyor-general sent over blank commissions for the appointment of deputy-surveyors among the arrivals. Two weeks later Halifax gave the Refugees permission to lay out town plots on both the "Parr-town" (east) and "Carleton" (west) sides of St. John harbour. On arrival with the June 1783 fleet Sarah Frost knew already that her Billy was to have a town lot measuring 40 feet in frontage by 100 feet.

By mid-summer the governor took the momentous decision of authorizing farm lots of 200 acres as an interim measure, subject to adjustment when London's instructions finally became known. He also bowed to practicality by agreeing that Loyalists might apply for land grants in groups rather than singly. Parr also took it upon himself to authorize Fort Howe commandant Gilfred Studholme to buy up all the lumber he could find for donation to the arrivals. At the same time he made the politically costly move of confirming that the Refugees of the Bay of Fundy Adventurers would be allotted the St. John Valley below the pre-Loyalist settlement at Maugerville, leaving most of the Provincials to the remoter reaches above.[5] This turned the military gentry, notably Edward Winslow, bitterly against the governor and was a key stimulus to Winslow's subsequent campaign to have the St. John Valley region made a separate colony.

Parr also acted early, and again bowed to practicality, by establishing a local leadership at Saint John. This caused no end of difficulty, as he complained to all who would listen. The Loyalists were strangers to the governor and their main settlements were far from Halifax. Their agents came recommended by the great Sir Guy Carleton, and Parr had little choice but to make them and their nominees magistrates, surveyors, and so on. This led to problems everywhere as appointees proved incompetent or corrupt.

"It has often happened to me here," wrote the governor defensively, "that a man has been recommended in the morning as a Worthy, honest, deserving Loyalist, one who has suffered greatly by Rebellion, a man to be intrusted, that I might depend upon his justice, honor, and integrity: the same day or next morning this worthy character is represented to me as the d____st villain breathing, a man destitute of every social virtue, not to be depended upon or trusted... [I]n this Situation what is to be done[?]" Parr had made "magistrates ...of men whom God Almighty never intended for the office, but it was Hobson's choice."[6]

The governor's most significant step in giving leadership to Saint John was to concentrate power in the hands of the commander of the Fort Howe garrison, Gilfred Studholme. Studholme was the obvious choice. Although an Irish professional soldier, he was a long-time resident at St. John harbour — he had even commanded the old Fort Frederick — and his value to government was attested already by the many civil appointments he held for Sunbury County. With no great financial stake in the settlement of the St. John Valley, he might be depended on to be fairly even-handed in his dealings.[7] As Surveyor-General Morris told him frankly, "The whole management of these and all other matters respecting those poor suffering Loyalists are left to your Management."

THE PRINCIPAL GENTLEMEN OF THESE LOYALISTS

So it was that Gilfred Studholme became the most important figure in the Saint John settlement in the days of Halifax rule. His central role in all matters civil and military made him a "kind of Chief Magistrate."[8] Beyond Studholme, leadership in 1783 and much of 1784 centred on a small core and a shifting circle of men. No one knew quite what their authority was. Sometimes they called themselves "Agents and Directors" and sometimes "Magistrates and Agents" and sometimes "Directors of the Towns at the Entrance of the River St. John."

In a loose sense this group originated with the agency for the Bay of Fundy Adventurers. The initial agents, who had gone through a form of election and been recognized by the commander-in-chief, co-opted others without further election. As noted earlier, these agents showed no doubt that their authority extended from New York to Nova Scotia, and in the short term any questioning of this authority was forestalled by the fact that Parr's administration treated them as if they represented the entire Refugee community.[9] In July 1783 the status of the emergent agents and directors gained legal reinforcement with Parr's appointment of several Loyalists to the Sunbury County bench of magistrates: James Peters, William Tyng, George Leonard, Fyler Dibblee and Ebenezer Foster. Each had voyaged northward in the May fleet, with charge of provisions on the ships in which they travelled. Peters, formerly of Orange County, New York, was the only official agent to accompany the first embarkation to Saint John. William Tyng was the former sheriff of Maine's Cumberland County. In occupied New York he had worked in the army commissariat's notoriously corrupt forage branch. He went to Saint John to take charge of the commissariat at Fort Howe, the function of which was victualling the thousands of arrivals. George Leonard, a Refugee from Boston, had been one of the most active and influential civilians at New York during the war. His role at Saint

John was such that he could claim "a principal Direction" of the settlement.[10] Fyler Dibblee was the Connecticut lawyer whose misfortunes were recorded in Chapter One. And Ebenezer Foster was formerly a substantial farmer and magistrate at Woodbridge, New Jersey. With Dibblee he was employed during June and July in compiling a report on the state of pre-Loyalist settlement along the St. John River.

Despite the hostility that many Loyalists would later direct at him, one figure who was not on site at the founding of Saint John was John Sayre. As secretary to, and practically head of, the New York Agency during the crucial spring and summer of 1783, the exiled Connecticut parson played a large role in arranging the departure of the first four fleets of Refugees for the Bay of Fundy. But Sayre himself did not arrive at Saint John until the latter part of August, and even then it is doubtful if he was influential in the direction of the place. Already, certain of his other activities, described in Chapter Three, had made him a controversial object of "contempt and neglect." Perhaps it was for this reason that he retired upriver to Maugerville, where he soon died.

More influential among the Loyalists leaders on site were Frederick Hauser and Oliver Arnold. Hauser had held the rank of captain in a small unit of Provincials known as the Loyal Foresters that surrendered with Cornwallis at Yorktown. As an agent, he was among the initial party sent northward in October 1782 to explore Nova Scotia for settlement sites. Although he set down initially at Annapolis, he was in and around Saint John in 1783 and 1784. As the only agent who knew how to run a survey, his practical skills were in demand. Oliver Arnold, formerly of Connecticut, and a lieutenant in the Volunteers of New England, travelled to Saint John in the May fleet. Almost immediately this youthful Yale graduate became local secretary to the agents and directors. For a time he was called the town clerk.[11]

Influential members of the Provincial military gentry also played a leadership role at St. John harbour. Only Major Daniel Murray of the King's American Dragoons was on site for an extended period in the summer of 1783, but several other prominent officers called in to pursue land speculations — notably Lieutenant-Colonels Abraham Van Buskirk and Isaac Allen, and Edward Winslow, the muster master general. The period between the arrival of the great body of Provincials in the autumn of 1783 and the spring of 1784 was when the former Provincial command-ers exerted greatest influence on the settlement. Various lists of agents, magistrates and directors also include the names of Lieutenant-Colonel Gabriel DeVeber and Major John Coffin. Yet the role of the military in early Saint John was less — proportionately — than that of leading Refugees because the chief military settlement was to be far up the river, around Sainte-Anne (Fredericton), where the Provincials would move as soon as practicable.

The term "agents and directors," referring to some or all of Studholme, Tyng, Peters, Leonard, Hauser, Sayre, Arnold, Foster, Dibblee and other civilians, with additions from the military gentry, was strangely ambiguous. If the source of the authority wielded by Commandant Studholme and Commissary Tyng is clear, that of other agents and directors is not. Some were members of the New York Agency, and some were justices of the peace, but these categories were not all-inclusive. Their real power over their charges derived from the fact that the provincial government made them its local embodiment. This gratified the expectations of leading Loyalists and perhaps comforted Governor Parr in the knowledge that, should the new settlements run into trouble, he would have scapegoats to offer the authorities in London.

ASTONISHING TOWNS HAVE BEEN RAISED

The Loyalists landed at St. John harbour angry, dispirited and vulnerable. They came not as heroic founders of a new nationality but as what Sarah Frost's journal calls "Loyalist sufferers." Many had fled their homes for a precarious existence in occupied New York. For them this was now a second exile. How could they regard themselves otherwise than as victims, the ineffably unfortunate casualties of two decades of British blundering, culminating in the ruinous terms of peace? "Was there ever an instance," demanded one devastated Refugee, "... can any history produce one, where such a number of the best of human beings were deserted by the Government they have sacrific'd their all for?"[12] Burdened by this self-image as victims, the Loyalists landed at Saint John certain that the British nation owed them a great deal. They came expecting and demanding the most tender solicitude. Once again they would sense betrayal. Fleet after fleet of exiles was precipitated on shore without so much as a shelter to go under, with no one ready to point out their promised lands. Despite everything, most remained.

Propaganda reports that had circulated at New York of the verdure and richness of the St. John Valley gave way to startling reality as Loyalist transport ships came to anchor. Although the interior reaches of the river were all that the advance party of the New York Agency had proclaimed, the prospect at St. John harbour was dank and depressing.

Everyone thought so. One contemporary called the terrain "very broken, barren and but little cultivated." Another spoke of the "rugged and tremendous precipices" that "deformed" the shoreline.[13] The grieving diarist Sarah Frost had seen nothing to equal it. Few physical features attracted favourable comment. One was the ice-free harbour. Another was the narrow, defensible entrance to the vast navigable stretches of the St. John River, which was guarded by a remarkable "reversing" falls.[14]

Climate united with geography to render early Saint John life dispiriting. Arrivals were hard-pressed to say whether summer or winter was the more disagreeable. Winter months were warmer than inland but so wet that there was no deep layer of snow to insulate primitive shelters. Bad weather set in early that first year. A volcanic eruption in Iceland made the winter of 1783–84 in the Maritime region the second coldest of the modern era. The clement months may have been even more disappointing. In mid-June the fog was still "so thick we could hardly see an inch — and our tea party crowded about the fire ... as if they were hearing stories of ghosts in the christmas holidays." Fort Howe commissary William Tyng complained that it rained three-quarters of the time.[15] Food spoiled, and the pestilential mosquitoes gained a breeding ground.

The single imposing feature on the horizon was the small group of buildings grandly called Fort Howe. If St. John harbour is viewed as a semi-circular arc, with the future settlement clusters of Parr-town and Carleton located on peninsulas on the east and west arms of the arc, then the Fort Howe hill falls about midway between. Erected as recently as 1778 on a commanding limestone cliff, it consisted of two blockhouses, an earthwork with eight cannon, a large house for the commanding officer and a barracks for one hundred men.[16] By the time the Loyalists arrived, much of the badly constructed fort was falling down. From its erection until late 1783 the post was garrisoned mostly by Provincials of the Royal Fencible Americans. On their disbandment they were replaced by a detachment of the 57th Regiment under Captain Elliott Ovens and then by two companies of the 54th Regiment under Colonel Andrew Bruce. Apart from the fort, the only human artifact to interrupt the landscape of greens and greys was a cluster of pre-Loyalist houses, huts and stores on Portland Point, at the base of the Fort hill.

Once the New York fleets arrived, this scene was transformed with a rapidity that amazed observers. When Sarah Frost landed at the end of June, Loyalists of the May fleet had put up only two huts. Soon, however, the military reported that astonishing towns had been raised. By March 1784 there were fifteen hundred framed houses and more than four hundred log cabins. Newspaper advertisements were locating tradesmen according to their "street." Not all early dwellings were rude. Court records reveal that in August 1784 Henry Nase hired a former sergeant in the King's American Regiment to build him a two-storey house, 20 feet by 18 feet, on the Carleton (west) side of the harbour. Four years later there were said to be upwards of two thousand houses, many of them spacious, and this at a time when many of the exiles had moved upriver to their farms. Observers often remarked how substantial the houses were for so new a town. The hurricane of 1787 blew ships ashore and sent Fort Howe's sentry boxes flying but damaged only a few roofs in the town.[17]

The spur to this remarkable building activity so soon
after arrival was the realization that few exiles would be able
to settle upriver on their promised land before the spring of
1784, combined with the fact that about mid-summer the
Nova Scotia government began supplying Saint John with a
modest allotment of building materials. An issue of 500 feet
of boards and 1,000 shingles per household was standard
in the twelve months for which detailed records survive.
In settlements thrown together without much planning
there were bound to be destructive fires. Four occurred in
a single week in June 1784, leaving dozens homeless. One
threatened the entire town, perhaps the same one called the
"Great Fire at Parr." [18]

Families who could manage it had carried food and livestock from New York. Pigs and poultry must have been the
most useful animals; cattle and sheep would require too
much forage. Those Refugees who arrived in the May and
June fleets might have sown seeds carried with them, but
only those who, like passengers on the *Union*, moved upriver
immediately could have expected to squat undisturbed on a
garden clearing until harvest.[19] The agricultural surplus of
the pre-Loyalist inhabitants upriver did not go far among
thousands of arrivals. The little food on sale at Saint John was
"extravagantly dear." Fresh meat was scarce. An entire settlement could not live on occasional rabbits, partridges and
pheasants. Bears learned to keep their distance, and moose
were soon so few that the first session of New Brunswick's
legislature would pass a conservation measure. Only fish —
notably cod, salmon and herring — were abundant in season.

With self-sufficiency in food impossible, Saint John's precarious lifeline was the army commissariat at Fort Howe. When

the May 1783 fleet arrived, the custodian of the nearly empty fort storehouse was local trader William Hazen. A few days later he made way for William Tyng. Tyng carried the burden of storing, distributing and accounting for the royal bounty of food until his superiors sacked him, perhaps to his relief, in December 1783. His successor, Loyalist Frederick William Hecht, had no better luck than Tyng at keeping the Refugees and Provincials satisfied; but his superiors gave him the benefit of the doubt they had denied his predecessor, and he kept his post during the arduous period through the end of 1785.[20]

Households drew full rations for members aged ten years and over and half rations for those under ten, so there was great incentive to exaggerate children's ages. The main issues were bread, flour, beef, pork and oatmeal, with small quantities of butter, oil, peas, raisins, vinegar, suet and salt distributed occasionally. The bread and oatmeal were substitutes for flour. Rations were barely sufficient for life. The experience of some of his men in the summer of 1783 moved Lieutenant-Colonel Isaac Allen to urge that something be done to assist those unable to purchase food: "[T]he soldiers Rations will not do, where a Man can procure no assistance from Labor or Plundering."[21] At first Loyalists were promised up to a year's provisions, to end in May 1784. Soon it was clear that this would not do, especially in view of the great delay in placing arrivals on their promised lands. Consequently the royal bounty of provisions was extended a further two years, first at two-thirds the rate in 1783 and 1784, and then at one-third. Beyond this, the very poor might appeal to the town's Humane and Charitable Society or to the Anglican church wardens for help from moneys raised at the annual Christmas day charity sermon.

Despite an acute lack of storage at Fort Howe and of small craft to move provisions up to Sainte-Anne (Fredericton), the food distribution was successful. There are individual stories of terrible suffering but no "food issue" developed in the public stores to compare with the intense land issue. Although both Tyng in November 1783 and his successor Hecht in November 1784 thought they were "inevitably ruined" by the non-arrival of provision ships, the only account of near starvation of a whole neighbourhood involved the Provincials who spent the first winter at remote Sainte-Anne.[22] Given the immensity of supply and distribution challenges this was no small achievement. To curb fraud in distribution of such a vast quantity of provisions through a primitive administrative system, the army appointed Thomas Knox to do a thorough muster, first of the Refugees and then of the Provincials. Knox found surprisingly little abuse, given that rations were issued to small parties at a time, the first Refugees who had settled upriver having to make the laborious journey down to Fort Howe every few months to be victualled.[23]

Although most settlers had access to rations, sickness and death were common at early Saint John, due to the crowding, the shortage of fresh water and firewood, the makeshift sanitation facilities, the inclement weather, the primitive nature of shelter, the limited supply of fresh food and the often low morale that were the lot of most. A particularly dramatic exit was that of Agent Fyler Dibblee. Ruined in prospects, burdened by debt and accused of embezzling public stores, Dibblee "took a Razor from the Closet, threw himself on the bed, drew the Curtains, and cut his own throat."[24]

There are many particular accounts of illness. Commissary Tyng's wife was so ill of fever and chills that in six weeks she only once made it to the door.[25] There are two stories of smallpox, three of measles and numerous testimonies to the baleful effect of damp and cold. Yet there were no epidemics. One impression of mortality is John Beardsley's notation that in the year ending October 26, 1784, he buried sixty-nine corpses.[26] This confirms that the settlements at the river's mouth were not visited by any contagion of epidemic proportion. Before long, the exiles would boast that their Loyalist Elysium had one of the healthiest climates in the world. Whether the story was of an old man fathering triplets, the production of a monster cauliflower or a harvest of salad greens in mid-April: all were hailed as proof that their new homeland was an Eden in the making.[27]

John Beardsley and James Sayre (brother of John Sayre) were the active Anglican clerics at Saint John during the first two years of the Loyalist era. They preached at both Parr-town and Carleton. John Sayre was present for a couple of months but was either so ill or preoccupied that he preached only once. Soon the temporary Anglican building was too crowded, and a proper church was built in time for consecration by Bishop Charles Inglis on his initial visit to the town in 1791. Newly consecrated Connecticut bishop Samuel Seabury also called in briefly to see old friends, and the charismatic Newlight Henry Alline saw enough of the place to pronounce the exiles spiritually "hardened" and "careless." Michael Kern, a Reformed minister, spent a few weeks at Saint John in the fall of 1783 before settling upriver. Among blacks the first preacher was Edward Morris. Though possessed of an official pass from the army at New York implying freedom, Morris and family had travelled to Saint John with the Georgia Loyalist Thomas Rogers, who claimed them as his property. Prior to lawyer Fyler Dibblee's suicide he seemingly coaxed several of Rogers's alleged slaves to desert the man for paid service elsewhere. It is Rogers's advertisement of their escape that reveals Morris as a "celebrated methodist preacher among the negroes."[28]

Physical and emotional hardship were the lot of most at early Saint John, but there were positive aspects of communal life too. Beginning in December 1783 the twin St. John harbour settlements could boast of a newspaper. The *Saint John Gazette*'s initial issues proclaimed business as usual on the part of numerous watchmakers, bakers and sailmakers, lately tradesmen at occupied New York. Other settlers advertised for students, brought in firewood from the country, ran ferries between the Parr-town and Carleton sides of the harbour, opened grog shops or wet-nursed to the gentry. "Every Body is Striving to do Something," boasted a Connecticut Refugee.[29] Traders who had entered exile with little capital struggled to recreate a transatlantic supply chain. Yet by 1785 the town had ten merchants specializing in dry goods, two in ship chandlery, five in foodstuffs and many more in general trade.[30] Uniquely fortunate was Thomas Pagan, who pocketed thousands of pounds from government for supplying boards and shingles for public distribution.

Like its commercial affairs, Saint John's social life commenced as soon as there were places where a few might gather together. For men, probably the chief recreations were hunting expeditions into the country and debating past misfortunes and present hopes over grog. By the spring of 1784 a Scots Friendly Society was off the ground, meeting at James Kirk's tavern in Parr-town's Lower Cove district. About the same time some professionals and artisans set about establishing a civilian lodge of Freemasons. It too met at Kirk's tavern, and its members would come to play a conspicuous role in the political affairs of the settlement. Both clubs gave generous support to members fallen on hard times. Less philanthropic was the Friendly Fire-Club, formed in 1785 by merchants and professionals at the Upper Cove for mutual assistance when a member's building caught fire.[31]

For the highest class of exiles and the officers at Fort Howe there were public and private assemblies. A "most Agreeable Ball" was held at the astonishingly early date of August 15, 1783. The high social season began about Christmas and continued throughout the deep winter. Although Parr-town and Carleton were little more than hamlets on the margin of a wilderness, their social leaders yielded nothing to Halifax in the sophistication of entertainments and elegance of costume. During Edward Winslow's first "season" at the new settlements, from 1785 to 1786, he resided at the aptly named Felicity Hall at the base of Fort Howe hill. To a leader of Halifax society he wrote with surprise that, "Till this winter I had no idea of the jollity & sociability which a good neighborhood may enjoy in the coldest of weather."[32] One such occasion was Queen Charlotte's birthnight in January 1786, when two dozen of the best families celebrated with dancing in the Fort Howe commandant's spacious quarters, followed by a very genteel supper.[33] The arrival of two Loyalist claims commissioners at the close of 1786 was a great spur to sociability.

We do not know who supplied music for the balls and private assemblies of the well-connected but perhaps the musicians included some of the "Banditti," the punning name for Saint John's string ensemble. Probably its leading spirit was Karl Schoenewolf, disbanded from the German Regiment du Corps. As well as playing second violin he imported "excellent manuscript overtures, symphonies, &c &c," which others then had copied. Among the Banditti were Jonathan Sewell and his younger brother Stephen. The Sewells were also the driving force behind the Forensick Society, an elaborate debating and self-improvement club that law students established in 1786. Towards the end of the decade the versatile Sewell boys took to the stage when the town inaugurated theatrical productions at the Mallard House tavern. Hannah Cowley's recent *Who's the Dupe?* and Susanna Centlivre's classic *Busie Body* formed the first bill. Both were tales of young women outwitting male schemes to marry them off unsuitably.[34]

At the opposite extreme socially and economically from the snug gentility of the Sewell brothers and Edward Winslow's Felicity Hall was a large class of Loyalists whose life was marked by oppression, failure or disarray. Most identifiable among this group were the free blacks. In the North America of the 1780s the notion of a black who was not a slave was a novelty, and perhaps it is not surprising that Governor Parr was moved to urge, "let them be considered as [part of] the human species (which by the by is not done everywhere)." The industrious, he suggested, should receive handsome lots of land.

Saint John's free blacks did share in the public bounty of lumber and land, but from the outset officialdom relegated them to the second class. Four companies landing in August 1783 were placed "at a little distance" from the main settlements.[35] Two years later, when Saint John opened the status of municipal freemen to its tradesmen, it excluded traders and artisans who were black. When New Brunswick held its 1785 election, the provincial Council denied blacks the vote. The 1786 provincial marriage law contemplated that blacks and "mulattoes," like Quakers, would contract marriage outside the official system, after customs of their own. Marginal in a different sense was the numerous class of "whites" responsible for nightly theft of provisions from the public stores and the many instances of criminal violence preserved in the settlement's court records. In addition to at least five taverns, enterprising Saint Johners provided the public with quite a number of "common ill-governed & disorderly house[s]," where patrons were wont to remain "drinking, tipling & misbehaving themselves unlawfully."[36]

I CERTAINLY EXPECTED TO FIND THE LANDS SURVEYED

Most forms of government assistance to Loyalists — clothing, blankets, tools, food, transportation, monetary compensation — generated some whining. But nothing compared to the indignation aroused by the maldistribution and nondistribution of the promised land. Disappointment arose on the arrival of the May fleet and dominated Saint John's public life for three years. Observers saw an anger so fierce they feared Parr-town and Carleton would slide into anarchy. Long after most exiles were clearing their farms, the land issue lived on politically as a mobilizing symbol of official betrayal. As such, it became the triumphant rallying cry of the opposition faction in 1785 at the colony's first general election.

One land issue was the perceived maldistribution of lots at Parr-town and Carleton in 1783 and 1784. Members of the May fleet had made some sort of preliminary division of Parr-town by mid-June.[37] Basic allocation was by lottery, though some agents and directors took choice commercial locations at Parr-town's Upper Cove for themselves and their connections. Agent John Sayre was "confident ... the People will not object to our having an exclusive Choice of Lands."[38] Sayre himself received both a prime lot in Parr-town and a house built at public expense even before he arrived. But apart from the few cases mentioned below, this initial June distribution of lots did not endure. Within two weeks there was a second fleet of exiles at Saint John, whose members expected town lots. In short, as George Leonard recalled, the town lots were "divided and subdivided on the arrival of almost every Fleet, to accommodate the Loyalists as they came, who were more numerous than was expected, until the Lotts of those who came first ... had been reduced to one sixteenth part of their former number of feet..." By the time formal grants were issued in August 1784, more than two thousand families had town lots, many of them allocated to the late-arriving Provincials.

Lottery continued to be the mode of lot distribution but was subject to evident qualifications. The draw was not for Parr-town and Carleton at large but on a district basis, so that arrivals in a particular fleet tended to get lots in the same area. Even within districts the number of fathers and sons who received adjoining lots confirms that the draw was not random. Less benign was the fact — apparent to anyone who plots on Paul Bedell's plan of Parr-town the lots awarded to the agents, directors and those who were later to emerge as leading government supporters — that men of influence received a major share of lots in the commercially attractive district known as Upper Cove. One summer arrival charged that the town lots were "unfairly and capriciously distributed and the best of them ingrossed by Mr. [George] Leonard and his confederates."

Suspicion of favouritism is reinforced by examination of the dates on which some Saint John Loyalists received their town allotment. Few of the original lot allocations survived to appear in the formal August 1784 land grant. Yet six of the final Saint John grantees held their designated lots from the summer of 1783: John Sayre, John Sayre Jr., George Leonard, George Leonard Jr., Gilfred Studholme and Jonathan Studholme Brownrigg.[39] The favouritism is unmistakable.

The case of Sarah Lester is a poignant instance of official partiality. This widow and mother of a large family drew 123 Germain Street, a fine commercial lot near Parr-town's Lower Cove. There she made improvements to the value of thirty-four pounds, "all she could collect from the wreck of [her] distressed circumstances." Then, in Lester's words, "the Directors of the Town, always alive to their own and their Friends Interest and deaf to the cries of the Widow and the Fatherless" awarded the lot to the son of Major Daniel Murray.[40] To many inhabitants, Sarah Lester's story represented a whole pattern of manipulation and venality stamped on the conduct of their agents and directors.

Misallocation of the town lots was not the main land grievance. Most exiles arrived at Saint John assuming that their promised farm land was being surveyed for immediate occupancy. "I certainly expected to find the lands surveyed and laid out, previous to my arrival here last

July," asserted an exile from the depth of his first Saint John winter. Hundreds more affirmed that "they expected ... land ... would have been located and survey'd for them according to their situation and Familys immediately on the arrival." "We were promised land," complained "Respectable Sergeants" of the disbanded Provincial regiments to Edward Winslow, their agent. "We expected you had obtained it for us." As it became evident that government had prepared no farm lots for immediate occupation, the exile community became intensely bitter. "[N]o lands being laid out for them distresses them beyond imagination," reported Commissary Tyng.[41] Most exiles were forced to sit out the growing season of 1783 and the winter stranded on town plots, building shelters that would be of no future use, expending savings in a place where prices were high and morale was low. For months together the exiles had leisure to reflect that again, in peace as in war, they had been victimized by their leaders.

What went wrong? Even as the Loyalists arrived Governor Parr was gathering evidence for the escheat process, authorizing Studholme to appoint surveyors, and directing the laying out of preliminary farm lots. But this accomplished little for the exiles of 1783. Only a few Refugees and no Provincials were on farm land at any time in 1783, and most of these, impatient at the delay, occupied as squatters. Surveyors, in theory paid by government but in reality unpaid for upwards of a year in some cases, demanded "presents" from those seeking their services. Loyalists unable to bribe them were apt to be ignored.[42]

A more significant source of delay was the total failure of co-ordination among the army bureaucracy, the New York

Agency and the Nova Scotia administration. Had Halifax been given timely warning of the enormous number of exiles due to arrive in 1783 and where they were planning to settle, and had the New York Agency or the army exercised the elementary forethought of sending surveyors ahead of the fleet, the worst of the land delay might have been avoided. But Parr was given practically no idea of when fleets would arrive, how many exiles they would carry or where they would go. Even under such circumstances, had the number of arrivals at Saint John been only a few thousand, adequate makeshift arrangements might have been made to locate them in 1783. With upwards of ten thousand arriving at St. John harbour, and even greater numbers elsewhere in Nova Scotia, ad hoc arrangements could not suffice.

A third source of delay in putting Loyalists on their promised land in 1783 was the slowness of the escheat process. At the earliest practical moment Parr began gathering evidence for the court proceedings necessary to cancel existing township grants along the St. John River for noncompliance with their terms, but the task took far longer than expected. The governor arranged that the only township proprietors actually resident — Hazen, Simonds and White — would not oppose escheat of their interests, but he had no such success with proprietors of other townships. These speculators, sensing that soon their vast, empty tracts would be valuable, opposed every stage of the law proceedings, so that escheat was accomplished only with great difficulty.[43] Obstruction was led by the proprietors' agent, the Nova Scotia attorney general, Richard Gibbons. As London's appointee, Gibbons was all but immune to Parr's displeasure.

It was for these reasons — problems with surveying, lack of coordination, the unexpected slowness of escheat — that so little progress was made settling the Loyalists in 1783.[44] Not until the spring of 1784 did the process of locating and granting begin in earnest. Within a matter of weeks most of those who wished could leave Saint John and Sainte-Anne and begin clearing farms. But problems remained, and even at the close of 1784 hundreds could protest they had "neither lotts or lands." Then, confusion attending the transfer of jurisdiction from Nova Scotia to the new administrators of New Brunswick slowed the process of turning surveys into land grants. The situation was compounded by the tardy arrival of the new colony's surveyor-general, George Sproule. Only in the summer of 1785 did land affairs on the St. John River correspond to the expectations of the Loyalists who had arrived two years earlier.

CHAPTER 3

MURMURING AND DISCONTENT

Just days from the landing of the May 1783 fleet, Fort Howe's commissary alerted his army superiors back at New York to "amazing discontents" among the people. He might have said the same at most points during the next three years. Canada's so-called "Loyalist City," and by extension the province of New Brunswick, began life in clamour and unrest.

Arriving exiles carried northward with them a heavy burden of grief and anger. In revolutionary politics the Patriots had outfoxed them. In war the generals had misdirected them. At the peace table their government had betrayed them. They came ashore wounded, reluctant and sullen. Hutted at the edge of a northern wilderness, most now faced a future of pulling stumps and shifting rocks, their children unschooled and unchurched. For people whose political instincts had been sharpened by a generation of revolutionary agitation, it's no wonder that, beginning just days after their arrival, Saint John Loyalists could display such truculence towards authority.

THEY APPEAR AT PRESENT TO BE IN A STATE OF ANARCHY

What great setback provoked amazing discontent among the first arrivals at St. John harbour?

For one thing, the Fort Howe commissariat was issuing blankets full of holes. They were so defective they would not cover twelve inches together. Although they were intended for discard, the army had given them to the New York Agency at the last minute, thinking they might be of some small use. As there were not enough to go round, the army added a number of whole ones. The good blankets were for families; damaged ones were for the single men. But no one explained any of this to the Refugees. When Commissary Tyng issued the blankets at Saint John, the unmarried men cried shoddy treatment — was this what Loyalists were now to expect? — and stirred the whole encampment to uproar. Back from New York came the army's angry order to issue no more blankets.[1] This primitive reaction — cutting off government aid — is an early hint that those in authority would be alarmed by criticism from Saint John Loyalists. It was too reminiscent of the overblown rhetoric that had led to rebellion in the old colonies.

Other signs from the early months of exile warned how easily discord might flare. Refugees in the May fleet balked at helping to land army food rations shipped northward, even though for their own use. Arrivals in the first four fleets refused to join in building provision storehouses unless paid exorbitantly. It was, claimed Commissary Tyng, a conspiracy "to pick the pocketts of Government." His first thought was to starve them into submission. Soon he was also threatening Provincial troops at the Fort Howe garrison with denial of rations unless they formed working parties, a threat that had some effect.[2]

Their experience in the old colonies did more than put arriving exiles into a combustible mood, so that even holes in blankets could spark unrest. One episode in particular, originating in New York City in mid-summer 1783, resonated for years in Saint John's long land controversy. In July, fifty-five Loyalists of the most respectable character, as they themselves declared, petitioned Guy Carleton, the commander-in-chief, for assistance in procuring farms of 5,000 acres in Nova Scotia. They required such estates, they urged, in order to regain their former standing in society.[3] Among these petitioners — in fact, one of the promoters of the scheme — was the very John Sayre who was at the same time secretary of the Bay of Fundy Adventurers. Three other Fundy agents were among the soon notorious "Fifty-Five." This looked very bad. Men responsible for the fate of thousands on the St. John River were attempting to build a special shelter for themselves against the risks of an exile's life.

No one familiar with the eighteenth-century world could be surprised at what the Fifty-Five proposed. Most were minor notables, and it would not have seemed indecent to favour them with a special allowance of land. Their presence in the exile settlements would add polish. True, they sought a larger acreage than official policy on land-granting permitted, but Nova Scotia was vast and almost empty. Carleton passed on their request to Nova Scotia Governor John Parr without objection. But less-well-connected Loyalists at New York showed no such gentlemanly spirit when word leaked out of what their betters were attempting. Meeting at Roubalet's Province Arms tavern they drew up a counter-petition of protest. Then they published a note inviting those still awaiting evacuation to Nova Scotia to call in and sign.[4] Hundreds queued up to do so.

These counter-petitioners claimed membership in that most woeful class of Loyalists — those who had fled within British lines from their original homes and now faced deportation into a second exile. They feared that the self-important Fifty-Five were scheming to get Nova Scotia's most desirable lands for themselves. This would force ordinary Loyalists to a choice between accepting remote and barren farm lands or submitting to be tenants of the mighty. Suddenly nervous at the furor among so many potential migrants to Nova Scotia, Carleton was at pains to soothe them. He would forward their protest to Parr. Now, he professed to doubt that any one person might receive more than 1,000 acres.

The controversy stirred by the counter-petitioners put an end to the land prospects of the Fifty-Five as individuals, but the political affair was only beginning. The panic of indignation that quickly produced 628 signatures of protest reflects the fragile psychology of the Loyalist community. It underlines how vulnerable they felt to official betrayal, particularly concerning land-holding and the status land carried. Among these counter-petitioners were many already signed up for evacuation to St. John harbour, including two dozen leaders of Refugee militia companies. They would carry their anxieties northward, where the affair of the Fifty-Five lived on for years as a mobilizing symbol of what many claimed was a conspiracy to reduce the rank and file of Loyalists to the status of landless "slaves."

Unrest over the conduct of those in authority also underlay a cluster of incidents at Saint John in the fall of

1783. People became suspicious that their agents were withholding government donations of clothing. Then, following the general landing of Provincial troops and families from the September fleet, Commissary Tyng noted that short rations of flour and bread had irritated a "lawless set of people" newly discharged from military discipline.[5] The most revealing sign of mounting popular alienation was a formal meeting at the end of October of Nathaniel Horton's militia company, Company 22. Horton's was one of the several dozen such bands of Refugees formed at New York to help smooth the migration northward, not for military preparedness. Twenty-eight heads of household were at St. John harbour by the time of this October meeting. One of their resolutions requested that Gilfred Studholme and John Sayre produce their documents of authority.[6] By what right, they demanded, did a garrison commander and agents for the Bay of Fundy Adventurers manage public affairs for the new settlement. Their complaints covered nearly everything — misapplication of clothing, blankets, building materials and charitable moneys. But the most urgent concern was favouritism in the distribution of farm lands and town lots. Like the counter-petitioners against the Fifty-Five of three months earlier, members of Company 22 feared becoming mere tenants, denied the right to vote. In aggressive and insinuating language they laid public blame for their grievances not on John Parr and the administration at Halifax but on their local agents and directors.

Winter was now approaching, and private letters sent from Saint John confirm that morale was fragile. One was penned by the ex-commander of Portsmouth's Fort William and Mary, John Cochran. Cochran wrote a fellow New Hampshire exile that the Loyalist encampment at St. John harbour was in a state of anarchy. Officers of the discharged Provincial regiments were insulted openly by the men they had recently commanded. In the whole settlement there was "nothing but Murmering and discontent," because the people were promised land but had none.[7] The exiles doubted that those lacking wealth or connections would ever get land. It seemed that once again, in peace as in war, their leaders were sacrificing the interests of the rank and file. How could there fail to be murmuring and discontent?

Cochran's pessimistic words confirm a similar assessment of Saint John affairs written a month later by Edward Winslow, the charismatic former muster master of Provincial forces. It is striking to see how closely Winslow's analysis — failure of leadership, grievance over land, drift toward anarchy — agrees with those of John Cochran and Horton's militia company. "The common people," warned Winslow, were "beginning to indulge themselves in all manner of excesses and (uncontrouled by the fear of punishments) they are becoming insolent & rude."[8] Their distress and insolence was caused by the delay in getting them out of crowded Saint John and onto the promised farm land.

By now Governor John Parr, too, was fretting over the clamorous mood of Nova Scotia's new settlements, especially Saint John. Ever sensitive to his own security, he tried to head off complaints that might reach his superiors by assuring the powerful Guy Carleton that most exiles at the St. John River were actually peaceable and quiet. Why, then, were there rumours of discontent? Parr saw it as the work of a handful of troublemakers. In denouncing them to

Carleton he mentioned for the first time the name of the
man who would lead Saint John's organized opposition in
1784 and 1785, a bold and factious attorney named Elias
Hardy.[9]

In fact, Parr's charge against Hardy was false. By late
autumn 1783 unrest was roiling in Loyalist Saint John without any prompting from the lawyer who was soon to be
vilified as the source of all discord.

A VERY TROUBLESOME FELLOW

The man possessed of a bold and factious disposition, and
falsely accused of instigating Saint John's political troubles,
had been born thirty-nine years earlier in southern England.
Elias Hardy practised law in London for five years before
migrating to Virginia in 1775, a place where he might
hope to occupy a large role on a small colonial stage. He
was still on board ship when he learned of the outbreak of
revolutionary fighting in Massachusetts. Soon the troubles
in Virginia closed the courts and Hardy survived by tutor-
ing in the family of Hugh Mercer, a Scottish physician at
Fredericksburg.[10]

What were Hardy's views on the American controversy?
As with most people who held an opinion, he opposed taxation without representation. This was a view that any loyal
subject might hold, but it must have pleased Dr. Mercer,
who was soon to become a brigadier-general in the rebel
army. Despite offers of employment in the Patriot service,
Hardy would take no part. The issue that finally divided
him from his Virginia friends was not the justness of the
American cause but the unjustified step of independence.
When Thomas Paine's *Common Sense* appeared in 1776,

urging and propelling Patriots to consider separation from Britain, Hardy denounced both the pamphlet and the idea. He escaped tar and feathers only by travelling through back parts of Virginia and Maryland until he found a navy ship that took him to safety at British-occupied New York City.

Here the obscure Hardy boldly offered his services to the commander-in-chief but was turned away, and he was never among the hundreds offered a temporary financial allowance. Had the army-Loyalist establishment courted Hardy rather than rebuffing him, early Saint John history might have been very different. As revolutionary troubles had closed the city's law courts, Hardy lived hand-to-mouth until commissioned as a public notary. He also joined the paramilitary Associated Loyalists. Perhaps it was this connection that introduced him to Martha Huggeford, who became his wife in October 1781. Martha was a daughter of Peter Huggeford, surgeon in the Loyal American Regiment and future captain of a militia company of the Bay of Fundy Adventurers. One of her relatives was a major in the Westchester Refugees.

Hardy's made his debut on the public stage in August 1782, when shocked Loyalists learned that Britain had begun peace negotiations by conceding colonial independence. A week after this incredible news became public at New York, eight Loyalists tried to channel popular anger in a constructive direction by petitioning the king that there be no final peace without guarantees for the safety of Loyalists and restoration of their property.[11] The petitioners were mostly well-connected merchants, lawyers, farmers and the future bishops Seabury and Inglis. That the eighth and final name among such worthies was Elias Hardy's reflects an impressive agility in using a moment of community upheaval to push himself forward.

His skill at self-advancement was again evident a year later when Loyalists awaiting evacuation uncovered the land-grabbing manoeuvres of the Fifty-Five. Hardy became a voice for the discontented as one of four men chosen at the Roubalet Tavern meeting to pen the savagely sarcastic counter-petition. This was despite the fact that his own law partner, John Roome, was a Fifty-Fiver![12] Hardy's leading role in the affair is attested by the fact that Charles Inglis, another of the Fifty-Five, denounced him later as "pursuing the same turbulent measures, and plaguing the poor Loyalists" in Nova Scotia as formerly at New York.[13]

But why did Hardy go to Saint John? He did not leave New York at mid-summer in Dr. Huggeford's Refugee company, of which he was a member. He was still there when word arrived that Parliament had voted financial compensation for Americans who had suffered losses on account of loyalty. Initially, such claims were to be lodged in London. In October Hardy and his partner Roome were advertising in the New York press that they would relocate to Britain and that Hardy would travel by way of Nova Scotia, from where he was prepared to carry claims to England for a fee of one guinea. On December 2, about a month after his arrival at Saint John, Hardy passed out handbills publicizing this agency and attracted a good deal of business. As in the case of the counter-petition at New York, he had found a way to turn common Loyalist misfortune into personal advantage.

By his own testimony Hardy arrived at Saint John in early November 1783, so he could not have taken part in, much less engineered, the Horton company's resolutions of discontent. Yet he must soon have become prominent in the grievance movement or Parr would not have misidentified him as its ringleader. Despite this, Hardy is best viewed as the most important of half a dozen leaders of protest. Those who came to prominence first were the printers William Lewis and John Ryan, whose weekly *Saint John Gazette* began publication on December 18, 1783. For nearly two years it was the only newspaper in the place and, judging by its surviving issues, was an ardent critic of the agents and directors. Early in 1784 Hardy's wife's brother-in-law Tertullus Dickinson and their Huggeford connections also became identified as spokesmen for dissent.

Within weeks of his November arrival Hardy offered to carry a statement of Saint John's grievances (probably those of Company 22) to Guy Carleton, now in England. In January 1784, with his departure nearing, this arrangement was formalized at a public meeting of the discontented at Charles Loosley's tavern in Parr-town. It appointed Hardy and others — soon dubbed the "anti-agents" — to represent Saint John's true situation to the powerful in Halifax and Britain and combat the lobbying influence of the agents and directors.

Hardy was gone from the St. John River by early February 1784. In his absence public criticism of the agents and directors became more varied and sophisticated, now that it had a forum in the press. Each of the surviving early issues of the *Saint John Gazette* prints some fiery denunciation of the community's administration. For example, on January 29 Lewis and Ryan published a highly readable sixty-line poem by *A Spectator*, identified as a resident of Carleton. Notable passages are grouped thematically below.

On Loyalist history:
By various scenes of fortune toss'd,
Lock'd up by one eternal frost;
An iron shore, ordain'd by fate,
For Loyalists their last escape;

A seven years war, a shameful peace,
Brings us no nearer a release;
Our prime and youth is quite decay'd,
Old age and poverty's display'd;
Friends and relations far from here,
And many things we held so dear;

On the mood of the Saint John Loyalists:
No recompense for service past,
The future too, an airy blast;
A piece of barren ground that's burnt,
Where one may labour, toil and grunt;

On the misapplication of Royal Bounty:
Pinn'd by a scanty meal of meat,
Donations promis'd, all a cheat,
Wrong'd by a set of ravilacs,
Of all but gun, and spade, and axe;

The choicest tracts for some reserv'd,
Whilst their betters must be starv'd.

A denunciation of agents and directors. The agents are referred to as "ravilacs," likened to a second Spanish inquisition, Pharaoh and Nero and consigned to the

Devil; John Sayre, secretary of the New York Agency
and also agent for the Fifty-Five, then dying of dropsy,
is denounced in terms of startling savagery. The agents'
object, observes *Spectator*, is to reduce ordinary Loyalists
to the status of slaves:

May he, the author of our woes,
Far fiercer than our rebel foes,
Have his due portion near a lake,
Which is ordain'd to such by fate;
May living worms his corps devour,
Him and his comrades fifty-four:
A scandal to both church and state,
The rebel's friend, the public's hate.

The main design that they're upon,
To keep us easy at St. John,
Till we have eat our bread and pork,
And then the D___l goes to work;
To them we'll go instead of Pharow,
But we shall soon behold a Nero;
To them we'll make our cries and moan,
Instead of bread they'll give us stone,
Except you'll give them all your living,
And every thing that's worth a giving;
Like slaves you cannot then resist,
Your lands likewise, except the Priests.

The *Saint John Gazette* followed with a lengthy dialogue
submitted by *A Plain Dealer*. Chiding the agents and their
detractors for bickering over the trivial matter of clothing

distribution, it focused on the failure to have lands escheated and surveyed during the previous growing season. Did the agents expect to find surveyors and instruments "growing upon the trees, or produced, as they wanted them, by magic"? *Spectator* had singled out John Sayre for special abuse; *Plain Dealer* turned attention to James Peters. In holding lotteries for town lots, Gilfred Studholme had refused to enter names into the draw unless certified by Peters (for Parr-town) or Richard Holland (for Carleton). In this role Peters had charged a fee and had excluded some people altogether. To *Plain Dealer* this raised anew the nagging question of authority: what right had the Bay of Fundy Adventurers or Guy Carleton or even the Crown to designate agents for the Loyalists of Saint John? Peters was a figure of whom it was easy to insinuate profiteering and favouritism because, like Sayre, he had been one of the Fifty-Five.[14]

Two of *Spectator's* themes reappeared in the *Plain Dealer* dialogue. One was the terrible charge that the agents and directors had obstructed early settlement of farm lands, forcing most to expend their money and allowances while they were stuck at Saint John, as part of a conspiracy to reduce the rank and file to the point where they must become tenants of the mighty. Like *Spectator*, *Plain Dealer* concluded that the only solution to Saint John's troubles was an appeal to Britain.

In its next issue the *Saint John Gazette* published yet another attack on the agents and directors, in the form of a letter from *A Soldier*.[15] Addressed to disbanded Provincials, it recited the by-now familiar land grievance.[16] But there was much more. Even viewed against the inflated language of the time, the letter's warnings of discontent, bribery, fraud, tenancy and "inevitable ruin" were sensational.

To understand why *Soldier's* words jarred the agents and directors to strike out at their enemies by using the law, it's necessary to call to mind the fragile civil authority in a settlement where the directors were regarded with suspicion and contempt. Already there had been an outbreak of fighting late in September 1783, reflecting disdain for the Royal Fencible Americans by soldiers of other Provincial units.[17] Then in December John Cochran had judged the community to be in a state of anarchy. In January Edward Winslow thought the disbanded Provincials had become "an irregular licentious body of men." The common people, he warned, were "becoming insolent & rude." Other observers hinted at troubling episodes of violence and expressed alarm for the public peace. Against this background of rising tension, the agents and directors might well take alarm at *Soldier's* dark threats. In this matter the authorities reacted with great efficiency, lending some credibility to *Spectator's* fear of a second Spanish inquisition. The day after publication, William Tyng and James White, as justices of the peace, forced Lewis and Ryan to give up the original of the letter and admit they'd received it from William Huggeford. Arrested the same day, Huggeford revealed that he had it from James Eccles,[18] a lieutenant in the disbanded Prince of Wales American Regiment. Eccles, when tracked down, admitted authorship and said he had left it at Dr. Peter Huggeford's. The magistrates put these facts before the grand jury, which charged William Huggeford and the two printers with publishing a seditious libel.

The *Soldier* affair is something of a landmark. In it the agents and directors used publication of the *Soldier's* rash letter to strike out at some of their most important critics.

In pressing for criminal prosecution, they introduced a corrosive theme that would persist in early New Brunswick politics: that criticism of local authorities amounted to sedition against the Crown. It was the ironic argument that a number of Saint John Loyalists were disloyal.

The events of early March also reveal something of their detractors. Apparently the magistrates chose not to prosecute the writer of the letter. Instead, they struck at Lewis and Ryan, who had made Saint John's only newspaper the mouthpiece of the anti-agents. Their investigative trail also led them to William Huggeford and to the house of Peter Huggeford, where the offensive letter had been left. Both were Hardy's in-laws.[19]

I HOPE WE SHALL SOON UNHORSE THE DOG

By the time of the *Soldier* affair, Hardy had been gone from Saint John about a month. Yet he scored a remarkable coup. He had sailed not for England but to Halifax, where he persuaded Governor Parr that there was enough merit in the charges against Saint John's managers to send Nova Scotia's chief justice to investigate. It would be naive to think that Hardy's lobbying was the only factor in Parr's decision. As he himself had never visited the St. John country the governor would have valued a firsthand appraisal from someone whose judgement he trusted. And by this time Parr had his own reasons for seeking to embarrass rather than uphold the agents and directors.

Parr was aware of an elaborate campaign in London to have mainland Nova Scotia made into a separate colony using unrest at St. John harbour as its pretext, a campaign that involved friends and allies of the agents and directors.

Perhaps he thought that one way to counter their assertions that Saint John's problems were the product of his own clumsy and remote administration was by gathering evidence to show that they were really caused by the agents and directors themselves.[20] It would be simplistic to think that Hardy alone was responsible for Chief Justice Finucane's mission, but it was a masterful turning of the tables on Saint John's appointed leadership.

Bryan Finucane reached Saint John about the middle of April 1784 and remained a month. Even before his arrival the chief justice had been damned as haughty, quick-tempered and tyrannical, an assessment with which the agents and directors would soon heartily agree.[21] Most unsettling was the fact that he came in company with Elias Hardy.

Finucane put up handbills warning people to stop building permanent shelters in case he should redistribute their house lots.[22] Then he looked into complaints against the agents and directors. Given the length of his mission there must have been a great deal to investigate, but the only charges to survive are twenty-nine recorded in the handwriting of Tertullus Dickinson, who was Hardy's wife's brother-in-law.[23] They concerned the size of town lots, plural lot-holding and the fact that some lot-holders were absentee.[24] To a striking extent the people whose holdings Dickinson attacked were agents and directors themselves, captains of Refugee militia companies and members of the military gentry. Little is known of Finucane's disposition of the charges, but the yelps of exasperation and humiliation he evoked from the agents and directors suggest he thought them well-founded.

In unpoliced new settlements, where the authority of the rulers was daily undermined by opposition from within, it was important that the chief justice be seen to accord magistrates, agents and directors the respect to which their position entitled them. Instead, true to character, Finucane carried on with "hauteur and parade." The much-maligned Studholme received "vile usage." George Leonard and fellow agents were summoned abruptly to answer charges of favouritism and misconduct that were nothing more than rumours from taverns and barbershops.[25] Under great stress, they assured themselves that Finucane's meddling would soon be undone and Hardy "thrown neck & heels, with his party, into the River." Hardy was clever but they would soon "unhorse the Dog."[26]

Both the chief justice and local officialdom regarded Finucane's mission to St. John harbour as a failure. With grim satisfaction George Leonard reported that divisions and complaints were worse than ever.[27] The agents and directors decided that the best defence to Finucane's inevitably hostile findings was an offence, and they petitioned for a hearing before Governor Parr and the Nova Scotia Council at Halifax.[28] The story their petitions told was framed as a power struggle with Elias Hardy and his network of upstarts. Should the opposition's men of low birth be appointed to public office then they, as gentlemen and men of honour, would resign.

Soon, however, Parr and Hardy combined to offer the agents and directors yet another public humiliation. In the latter part of June, Parr appointed a board to investigate the distribution of land, lumber and other government donations to the settlers on the St. John River.[29] Four of the commissioners were former officers in the disbanded Provincial regiments.[30] The fifth was Elias Hardy. But the board's appointment lasted little more than a month. Parr withdrew its mandate abruptly when word reached Halifax at last that the game was up. Six weeks earlier the British government had formed the St. John region into a separate colony. The revocation came following a two-day hearing before the provincial council granted to the agents and directors at the end of July. Championed by Lieutenant-Governor Edmund Fanning, a North Carolina Loyalist, the directors were judged to have managed Saint John affairs fairly and properly. Then, in a stunning reversal, the provincial secretary warned Elias Hardy formally that matters of governance at Saint John belonged to the agents and directors, "without the interference of any other person whatever."[31]

To this point the obscure Hardy had scored remarkable successes with the governor at Halifax. Aided by a sympathetic Parr, he might soon have brought matters at Saint John to the crisis that would have given the governor reason to dismiss the agents and directors. Now, all efforts by both agents and anti-agents, in Saint John and in Halifax, were overtaken by the decree from London. Separation of the St. John region into a new province changed everything.

Defeat of the Hardy faction was not the work of the agents and directors themselves. It was a consequence of London's decision to free the St. John River country from Halifax control. Communication with Britain was so slow that little of Saint John's political troubles in early 1784 can have influenced London's thinking. In a further sense the mid-summer triumph of the agents and directors proved a hollow one. When senior appointments were made to the government of the new colony, those who had actually settled at St. John harbour, enduring insults from malcontents and worrisome duplicity from Governor Parr, were passed over in favour of claimants whose influence was greater and who had done their politicking in London rather than the wilds of Nova Scotia. It was this latter group who would monopolize New Brunswick's official loaves and fishes for more than a generation.

The idea of organizing one of Britain's remaining territories into an asylum for loyal exiles had been talked about for years. Everyone agreed that the American controversy had spun out of control largely because Britain had left the executive branch of colonial government too weak and had allowed local societies to evolve too far from the model of the parent state. In that sense, a projected Loyalist colony would be framed on counter-revolutionary lines. It would have a strong executive, a robust local aristocracy, an army garrison, a state-supported episcopal church, a church-dominated college and a judiciary dependent on the Crown for tenure and insulated from democratic financial control.[32] While the thirteen new republics to the south sank into democratic anarchy, this Loyalist colony, ordered on firm, hierarchical lines, would become the flourishing "envy" of the American states.

THE GRANDEST FIELD FOR SPECULATION THAT EVER OFFERED

"Take the general map of this province," exulted Edward Winslow on a visit to the St. John River in July 1783, "…observe how detached this part is from the rest — how vastly extensive it is. [N]otice the rivers, harbors &ca. [C]onsider the numberless inconveniences that must arise from its remoteness from the Metropolis [Halifax] & the difficulty of communication. Think what multitudes have & will come here — and then judge whether it must not from the nature of things immediately become a separate government."[33]

He followed by urging his correspondent, Ward Chipman, to migrate from New York to England rather than Nova Scotia, where he would be well placed to promote this vision of a new colony on the western shore of the Bay of Fundy.

Winslow's is thought to be the earliest speculation that the St. John region might be separated from Nova Scotia. Barely eight months later London's decision was made. This implies a relation of cause and effect — that it was the partition movement that produced the partition. That conclusion is at least doubtful.[34] In the wake of the lost revolution the British were strangely willing to bear the cost of governments for new colonies with very few inhabitants. They might have been disposed to wean the St. John Valley from peninsular Nova Scotia regardless of lobbying, and it is certain that Winslow's best propaganda cannot have reached London until after the decision was made.

The politics of Winslow's partition campaign as it impinged on the politics of Saint John was a game with four sets of players and strategies: the partition lobbyists in London, inspired from Halifax by the restless Edward Winslow; the agents and directors; Governor John Parr in Halifax; and the Hardy faction at St. John harbour.

THE PARTITION LOBBY

The partition dream conceived in Edward Winslow's fertile imagination as he toured the St. John valley in mid-summer 1783 was born of personal ambition. Worried about his own future in the wake of the lost war, Winslow foresaw that "private ambition & private interest" would now become the dominant motivations. In 1783 and 1784 he, Chipman and their soon-to-be unemployed friends of the Provincial military were scrambling to recover the sort of security into which they felt they'd been born. Winslow spoke for many when he despaired that at war's end his prospects were blacker than hell. In the enthusiasm for a separate Loyalist province that took hold of him suddenly at the St. John River, he saw a means to distinguish himself by proposing a plan that amounted to the "grandest field for speculation that ever offered."[35]

Although Winslow conceived the partition dream in the summer of 1783 and was bold enough to propose that Chipman place himself strategically in England to advance the cause, no partition campaign became realistic until the beginning of 1784. By that time it was known even in England that Saint John Loyalists were discontented, presenting an opening to propagandize against the administration of Governor Parr. More importantly, Winslow had converted his politically well-connected military superior, Brigadier-General Henry Fox, to the view that partition of Nova Scotia was critical to the success of the Loyalist experiment and that Fox himself should become governor of a separate St. John territory. In January Fox arrived in England armed by the busy Winslow with maps and papers and willing to exert his considerable influence in the cause.[36] Winslow himself provided comrades in England with a stream of spirited partition arguments. Their theme was Halifax's responsibility for the desperate and confused situation at the St. John River.

THE AGENTS AND DIRECTORS

By March 1784 the British government, from whatever combination of motives, had decided on partition. From

London, Ward Chipman reported that separation was beyond doubt. Stranded at Halifax, Winslow did not hear the glorious news for some weeks, and even then the British took an agonizingly long time formalizing the decision. Fearful that his coup might yet fail, Winslow broadened the campaign by appealing to the agents and directors at Saint John to send a pro-partition address to London.

Of all the Saint John Loyalists it was the agents and directors who had least reason to be dissatisfied with Parr's oversight of the region. It was to him that they owed their position. But by the end of April, Chief Justice Finucane was at Saint John scrutinizing their conduct, undermining their authority and flattering their critics. It was clear that Parr was preparing to rebut Winslow's partition propaganda by showing that the source of trouble was the misconduct of local leaders. It was only natural that the agents and directors would now cast their lot in favour of partition. They complied with Winslow's plea for a pro-partition address and passed along a similar message to the managers of the St. Andrews settlement in the Passamaquoddy region, who produced a petition of their own.[37]

In embracing partition, the directors' concerns were three: embarrassing Parr and Finucane, ridding their settlement of Halifax's control, and outflanking the Hardy faction. All are reflected in a libellous screed against Elias Hardy that George Leonard circulated in early May, while Chief Justice Finucane was still investigating at Saint John. It originated in a letter to Leonard from Joseph Aplin, a Rhode Island Loyalist in Edward Winslow's circle at Halifax. It was intended, said Aplin, to destroy Hardy's credibility with his own supporters.[38] Leonard and colleagues were so rattled by Finucane's ongoing mission that they made the mistake of circulating Aplin's charges openly. Hardy at once turned the matter against them by publicizing the affair in the Saint John and Halifax press, to the embarrassment of Winslow, Fox and the partition movement generally. Later, he sued Leonard for defamation.

GOVERNOR PARR

"I have a most unpleasant difficult game to play." So wrote a defensive John Parr, twice on one summer day in 1784.[39] His game image was well-chosen. For those caught up in the politics of partition, the shifts in attitude and rhetoric and the gaps between official posturing and private candour suggest a keen attention to gamesmanship. No one found it more important to separate public and private attitudes than Parr. Prudence and dignity required that he take no public stand on partition, so that he might adjust himself to any outcome. He did not even raise the subject with the British government until he knew of its decision.

Yet privately Parr could not be neutral. By early 1784 he must have known that General Fox would launch an active campaign in England, the chief argument of which would be that Saint John's troubles were the result of ineptitude by Halifax authorities. If such arguments won creation of a new colony, Parr would suffer the humiliation of having his jurisdiction reduced by half. He might lose his job altogether. What the governor needed was a way to work against partition quietly. It came to him in February 1784 when he met Elias Hardy, a brother Freemason, who was visiting Halifax on his mission of grievance. In Hardy's charges against the agents and directors Parr sensed a chance to undercut the chief pro-partition argument by showing that the troubles at Saint John were the fault of the local magistrates themselves.

Parr needed only to send an investigator to Saint John to enquire into the source of discontent, a move consistent with his duty as governor. If Hardy's complaint proved sound, the case for partition would be discredited. When Chief Justice Finucane returned to Halifax from Saint John he brought word that the agents and directors had prepared a public address favouring partition, that the Aplin letter circulated by Leonard had charged Parr with working against partition and that Hardy was opposing the work of the partitioners. By this time Parr must also have heard rumours from England that the British government was considering the question of a separate colony. That may explain Parr's bold new attack on the agents and directors. He created a short-lived Board of Inquiry to look into grievances on St. John River and made Elias Hardy a member. He also sent Andrew Finucane, brother of the chief justice, to London to lobby against partition directly.[40] Simultaneously, the chief justice himself wrote details of the situation at Saint John to one of his own English contacts. As with Parr, his object was supplying allies with the means of countering the partition lobby.

Parr's conduct towards all aspects of the Loyalist question between 1782 and 1784 was governed by an overriding concern to save his new job, and he played his self-styled game with skill. When word did reach Halifax in July that the partition campaign was won, Parr was positioned to accept defeat without public loss of face. He participated in the exoneration of the agents and directors by the provincial Council and even broke his official silence on partition by writing on it favourably to the British government. It was all part of his game.

THE HARDY FACTION

Elias Hardy did not work openly against partition, though probably he wanted to. He knew that partition would amount to a great victory for the agents and directors in Saint John's internal political struggle, freeing them from Halifax's meddling and reversing the rise to influence of his own circle. Partition would put him and his allies again at the mercy of the magistrates in a settlement where, as the *Spectator*-poet had complained, "prosecutor sits as judge." Yet Hardy denied more than once that he had actually worked against partition. What he did oppose was the conduct of the partitioners, and he did his best to frustrate their effort to supply Edward Winslow with a pro-partition address for use in London.

The agility with which the Hardy faction endorsed the general idea of partition while damning the partitioners reflects the high stakes. For all sides in the partition game, the primary motive was achieving or hanging on to personal security. Victory, when it came, went to Edward Winslow's circle, who would become the rulers of the new colony. The main losers were Hardy's connections, who were marginalized from power once again.

THE EXCESSIVE JOY CANNOT BE DESCRIBED

New Brunswick was created on June 18, 1784. Discreetly, the British attributed separation to the great distance between the St. John River and Halifax. Three weeks later Colonel Thomas Carleton kissed the king's hands to become the first governor.[41] With his new bride he stepped ashore at Parr-town on Sunday, November 21, at about three o'clock in the afternoon. Saint Johners received them with three huzzas, three cheers, two seventeen-gun salutes and an "excessive joy" beyond description. To cries of "long live the King and the Governor" Carleton walked to the house of George Leonard, the controversial magistrate, where he made a temporary home.

One of the rituals of eighteenth-century public life was the reading of an address to a great man on a great occasion. The one presented to Carleton describes its signers as oppressed and insulted Loyalists who looked to the governor to deliver them from tyranny and injustice.[42] On the surface, this referred to Patriot oppression during the war. In context, it was a sneer directed at Parr, Finucane and Halifax officialdom. Typical of the man, Carleton's reply was colourless, promising only a just and upright administration.

The new governor's appointment gave real cause for joy to Saint John and the clusters of Loyalists around Sainte-Anne, Passamaquoddy and Cumberland. A colonel in the 29th Regiment during the Revolution, the Anglo-Irish Carleton was a younger brother of the esteemed Guy Carleton, the former commander-in-chief. He had spent much of his early military career on the continent of Europe. A decade before landing at Saint John he served with the Russian army, battling "with the Turks on ye lower Danube." However, his service in the American war had been undistinguished, and he was fortunate to be offered the New Brunswick posting after two others turned it down.[43] It was an open secret that his appointment might be only temporary, until the popular Henry Fox could be persuaded to take the job.

Few were to question that Carleton gave New Brunswick the just and upright administration promised in 1784. Honest, sober, religious, plain in dress, generous with his private means, he was genuinely sympathetic towards the plight of his impoverished charges. Contemporaries noticed with approval that he spent his entire official income within the colony. Such contrasting observers as William Cobbett and Bishop Inglis agreed in praising his personal virtues.[44] Yet Carleton's "temporary" direction of New Brunswick lasted thirty-three years and gave all concerned cause for dissatisfaction. Austere by nature (he was a prodigious walker)[45] and inclined to the military life, he proved a mediocre political leader. Enemies lampooned him as "Simple Tom" and said he was a tool of his advisors.[46]

Also arriving in November 1784 and for some months after were the men who would shape the official life of New Brunswick for upwards of a generation. The most fortunate were those with salaries paid from the British treasury: Provincial Secretary Jonathan Odell (of New Jersey); Chief Justice George Ludlow (New York); Attorney-General Jonathan Bliss (Massachusetts); Surveyor-General George Sproule (New Hampshire); and the three junior judges, Isaac Allen (New Jersey), Joshua Upham (Massachusetts) and James Putnam (Massachusetts). Less adept in the scramble for glittering patronage prizes were Edward Winslow and Ward Chipman (both of Massachusetts), who had to content themselves with unlucrative titles as surrogate-general and solicitor-general respectively.

If merit had counted for little when London filled the richest posts in the new colony, neither did actual service at the St. John River. Of those named, only Allen and Winslow had ever set foot in the territory that became New Brunswick. Notably, those who had toiled for eighteen months to manage Saint John during the troubled time of Nova Scotia rule were passed over, to a man. The most that some of the now-supplanted agents and directors received was a seat on the province's council, where service was unpaid. Their fall into "nothingness" was dramatic.[47]

Members of the new office-holding elite were keen enough to leave England, even for the wilderness of the St. John River. The thousands of Loyalists who had fled America for Britain felt distressingly out of place. In the colonies a Ludlow or Bliss or even a Chipman had been a figure of some importance. At the hub of empire he was "lost," "Nothing" and his contemplation of his obscurity was "Vexation of Spirit." Ward Chipman spoke for many when he wrote from London that he'd rather have a decent income in New Brunswick than live amid the wealth of England.[48] At one level, then, the official elite were looking for restoration of their former standing in society. They hoped to strut on a small stage, saluted as honourable and esquire. In the Lilliputian world of New Brunswick their favour would be sought, their opinion deferred to, their sons called gentlemen and their daughters genteel. On Edward Winslow's first visit to Saint John he experienced the immense gratification of regaining his former status in the world. No one sought governmental favours without first courting his recommendation. This gave him "vast pleasure."[49] Winslow and his circle hoped to live out their days where what he called the common people would be obedient and grateful subjects.[50] New Brunswick was to be not only, as the colony's motto proclaimed, a *spem reduxit* — a restoration of hope — for despairing Loyalists on the St. John River, but also a restoration of the hopes, careers and fortunes of those chosen to govern it.

Creation of the Loyalist colony represented more to the elite than financial and social renewal. It was their chance to vindicate those principles of empire and authority for which they had been martyrs in the revolution. It was their chance to prove to the world and to themselves that a British colony ordered on firm, hierarchical principles would flourish and become the envy of its republican neighbours. If the New Brunswick experiment succeeded it would prove them right before all generations. If it failed it would mean they had fought the revolution in vain. To those tasked with founding a new society in the wilderness, theirs was an errand of mythic proportion. With elegant and revealing symbolism Ward Chipman chose as Saint John's civic motto Aeneas' exclamation on sighting the new city of Carthage: *O fortunati, quorum iam moenia surgunt!* (O fortunate ones, whose walls rise up already!). In the same spirit Edward Winslow proclaimed that the constitution of this unique colony would be "the most Gentlemanlike one on earth."[51]

New Brunswick's rulers came to their task inspired by the romantic self-image that, like the exiled founders of ancient Carthage and Rome, they were called to the work of heroes. They had demanded creation of a Loyalist colony. Now, Aeneas-like, they staked political and psychological redemption on its success.

CHAPTER 4
REPRESENTATIVES OF THE PEOPLE IN OPPOSITION TO THE PEOPLE

"Long live the King and the Governor!" This was the hearty shout from thousands as Thomas Carleton stepped ashore at St. John harbour in November 1784.

Just a year later, in the heat of New Brunswick's first election campaign, Saint Johners were drinking their beer to cries of "damnation to the Governor and Council." Soon, many would declare their disappointment so great that they feared a *new* American revolution — at Saint John.[1] Carleton's regime struck back in panic. It condemned these words as seditious. It jailed those who circulated them. It outlawed petitions for correction of public grievances. It tarred its political enemies with the detestable name of rebel. The transformation from American Loyalist to colonial New Brunswicker had begun.

SECURING OF A PERFECT OBEDIENCE
Eighteen months of rule from Halifax, carried on though agents and directors, had reduced the exiles at St. John River to near anarchy. Now Governor Carleton and his Council

of advisors hurried to right the affairs of their new province. Their priority was land. In that first full year, the Council met almost daily to hear 1,700 petitions on land matters alone. Most applicants only wanted their promised tract of the wilderness, but many situations were complicated. Hasty surveys had sometimes left two families with overlapping claims, leaving the Council to play the role of Solomon. Others complained that their assigned lot was hopeless for farming or, if a town lot, unsuited to commerce, and asked for another. The Council's work was hindered by unfamiliarity with the province, lack of accurate maps and the delayed arrival of the new surveyor-general.[2]

The most important decision of Carleton's early administration came at once — chartering the twin settlements of Parr-town and Carleton as a city. They called it *Saint John*, echoing the name given by Samuel de Champlain in 1604. Saint John's new civic government was based on New York City's charter of 1731. Why New York? Under the New York model, the important city office-holders were not elected locally; they were appointed by the provincial Council. For mayor and deputy (recorder), Carleton chose Gabriel Ludlow (brother of the chief justice) and Ward Chipman, the solicitor-general. For the critical first year the aldermen, too, were appointed.[3]

From the outset of settlement, some Loyalists at Saint John had pressed Governor Parr for civic incorporation. Carleton's granting it now removed the town from direct control by the justices of the peace, many of them controversial former agents and directors. But this was not his real motive. In the very charter creating Saint John he pointed to the evils plaguing the "upright" part of the community for want of an orderly local government. To Carleton the attractive feature of city administration on the New York model was its court system, run by an appointed mayor and recorder. This arrangement, he assured his superiors in London, would soon bring the people into "perfect Obedience." It would reclaim the multitude through a "vigorous police."[4]

The Council's decision to erase "Parr-town" from the provincial map and replace it with Saint John signalled more than disdain for the days of Halifax rule. Even in toponymy — choosing place-names — a Loyalist province would stand apart from its neighbours. Voyagers along New Brunswick's Bay of Fundy coastline encountered a High Anglican constellation of saints — St. Stephen, St. David, St. James, St. Andrews, St. George, St. Patrick, Saint John, St. Martins. Saintly place names were nearly unknown in colonies settled by religious Dissenters, such as Massachusetts and Nova Scotia. For New Brunswick's eight counties the provincial executive chose mostly English names, and it subdivided them into Anglican-sounding "parishes," not the townships of Nova Scotia and New England usage. Carleton and his circle associated townships with local democracy and disorderly public meetings. New Brunswick's parishes would be run by officers chosen by the county magistrates, all of whom in turn were appointed by the provincial Council and could be dismissed at any time. As with Saint John, each county received its anti-democratic charter by the governor's decree, before the legislature first sat.[5]

In February 1785 Carleton toured population clusters up the St. John River and decided to fix New Brunswick's future seat of government at Sainte-Anne. It was an abandoned Acadian hamlet being settled by disbanded Provincial soldiers. In honour of the Duke of York, George III's second son, he named the intended capital "Frederick'stown."[6] But why not make Saint John the capital? Carleton maintained that a seat of government more than 60 miles inland would be less vulnerable to enemy attack than one on the coast. It would also spur settlement of the colony's magnificent interior. As well, the eighteenth-century mindset regarded inland towns as more virtuous than seaports. Government and the Supreme Court finally removed upriver to Fredericton at the end of 1786. By then, events at Saint John made Carleton's choice of a distant capital seem wise indeed.

For many months after the governor's arrival there was no sign of dissatisfaction with the new order. Loyalists looked to Carleton with genuine hope. Perhaps some leaders of the former dissent even had it in mind that the regime would find a use for their own talents. What did not fade was the desire for revenge on Saint John's former agents and directors. A month after Nova Scotia's Council exonerated them, David Melville, former secretary of Elias Hardy's committee of correspondence, published an elaborate attack. It took the form of "Proposals, for Printing … an accurate History of the Settlement of his Majesty's Exiled Loyalists."[7] The history Melville proposed, said to run to three hundred pages, would detail how corruption and incompetence had delayed the settlement process, stranding thousands in idleness and despair. Ominously, Melville promised to show "the probability of this settlement being brought under subjection to the united states if the leaders are not closely watched."

Elias Hardy and his Huggeford relations also found ways to keep alive their association with the old protests while advancing their personal claims to attention. In the early days of Carleton's rule, both Peter Huggeford (Hardy's father-in-law) and Tertullus Dickinson (Mrs. Hardy's brother-in-law) petitioned to have the town lots awarded them by Parr and Finucane in the preceding spring turned into formal land grants. Carleton refused.[8] Huggeford was also behind a petition to the governor signed by 345 fellow Saint Johners. In colourful language it retold the story of misconduct and suspected corruption by the former agents, not omitting a jab at the old Fifty-Five. For his part, Hardy introduced himself to the governor by handing in a list of vacant lands he thought the Crown could reclaim and open for settlement. Assigned to investigate, Solicitor-General Chipman found that there was nothing in it. Carleton did extend an olive branch by offering Hardy an appointment as Saint John's city clerk. He refused.[9] He was not ready for co-option.

By the autumn of 1785 Carleton could reflect on his progress with satisfaction. The last of those intending to farm were on their promised land, and his Council had a system in place for resolving disputes. Departments of government were functioning. The whole province was divided into counties with three dozen parishes, and Saint John had a civic administration. A Supreme Court had opened, inaugurated with an "excellent and pathetic" charge from Chief Justice Ludlow. Missionaries and schoolmasters of the Church of England were locating in the major settlements, attending to education and morality. The royal bounty of provisions was keeping many on their clearings who might otherwise drift back to the land of rebellion, with extra rations for the truly needy.[10] Above all, Carleton had introduced a spirit of "decorum and industry" where formerly there was chaos and discontent.

Missing from these accomplishments was the convening of a provincial legislature. As Carleton took leave of England in August 1784 his superior suggested that New Brunswick was already populous enough to hold an election. Once on the spot he made no haste to comply. For the interim his official instructions authorized carrying on public business by decree of governor and Council.[11] Although Carleton denied any intention of letting such dictatorship extend to matters — such as taxation — normally reserved for an elected body, he was quite determined to lay down the basic lines of provincial organization without meddling from elected representatives of the people. The less an assembly had to do, he reasoned, the less would be the risk of the fatal "American spirit of innovation" taking hold in the Loyalist colony.[12]

By autumn 1785 the governor could postpone elections no longer. Given the political quiet of the colony, there was no reason to delay the inevitable. Further procrastination might alarm the people, who had been without elected government in their former colonial homes in many cases for nearly a decade, and it would be hard to justify to London. In a colony without roads, the legislature could meet only in the early months of the year when travel on the frozen St. John River was possible. To convene a legislature in early 1786, elections would have to take place towards the end of 1785.

One factor may have sealed Carleton's resolve to act. In mid-October the first number appeared of the *Royal Gazette*. It was to be published weekly by Christopher Sower, now

"Printer to the King's Most Excellent Majesty." With a sneer at Saint John's existing newspaper, the new king's printer vowed to publish only what would promote "good Order and Morals" and to reject anything intended to serve "Party" purposes or "Disrespect to Government." In the pompous Sower, latest in a line of Pennsylvania German printers, the governing elite gained an ally willing to counter the unsettling influence of Lewis and Ryan, who had done government printing to this point. As with much in the politics of early New Brunswick, the rivalry that now sprang up between the *Royal Gazette* and the *Saint John Gazette* was continued from Loyalist New York, where Sower had printed the tri-weekly *New-York Evening Post* and Lewis and Ryan, the weekly *New-York Mercury*.[13]

HUZZA FOR THE LOWER COVE!

Four days after the *Royal Gazette*'s debut, Carleton ordered the eight county sheriffs to conduct elections for a House of Assembly that would convene early in 1786. Sanford Oliver, high sheriff of the city and county of Saint John, announced that voting would begin on November 7. Saint John, the most populous county, would choose six of the Assembly's twenty-six members. Because many settlers actually on their land had not received formal grants, it was impractical to restrict voting to freeholders. Instead, all white adult males resident in their county for three months could vote. This represented a nearly universal manhood suffrage and it may have been without precedent in the North Atlantic world. Explaining this startling indiscrimination to London, Carleton offered the hope that he would nonetheless secure a compliant and respectable assembly.[14]

In the main his hope was fulfilled. In Westmorland County, Acadian Roman Catholic voters were harassed, but in York nearly eight hundred men assembled for polling with "no appearance of riot, no violence or insult." In Kings County the election was notable only for the display of "one of the most magnificent Flags, ever seen in America," handiwork of the irrepressible Charles Loosley. But Carleton had miscalculated the political temper of the Loyalists living around him at Saint John. Even a newly-arrived Anglican minister writing in the week of the election call could see that "the people are split into parties, and divided in sentiments, passions, & interests."[15] The local campaign generated not just flags, party badges and election handbills but sticks, brickbats and bludgeons. It was marked by a short-lived triumph of the revived opposition faction followed by its systematic suppression by the governing elite.

The Saint John press speculated that sixteen names would be offered in the local election, but only twelve of them were nominated before Sheriff Oliver at a public meeting on November 7. Six candidates formed a pro-government slate headed by Attorney-General Jonathan Bliss and Solicitor-General Chipman. Six comprised an opposition ticket led by Tertullus Dickinson.[16] In popular shorthand, the government candidates were the "Upper Covers," named for the area of the Parr-town peninsula where the influential held a disproportionate share of commercial lots. In the late eighteenth century, taverns were informal political nurseries, so it's not surprising that the Upper Covers chose Mallard House as their headquarters. In contrast, Dickinson's slate were known popularly as the "Lower Covers," and they too had a tavern headquarters, Charles McPherson's coffee house.[17] Missing from the Lower Cove ticket was the name of Elias Hardy. His name was absent because an influential friend was sponsoring his election in sparsely populated Northumberland County.[18] It was natural that he should prefer a safe seat in Northumberland to a Saint John contest against the law officers of the Crown, particularly as it meant that seven rather than six Lower Covers might win seats in the assembly. When Hardy was declared elected on November 17 he had the satisfaction of out-polling a pro-government ticket consisting of George Leonard and Stanton Hazard, two of his political enemies from Saint John. Like Hardy, they were running in remote Northumberland as non-residents.

At Saint John voting began on November 7 at McPherson's tavern, after the nomination speeches, and was to continue from noon to 4 p.m. daily until Sheriff Oliver decided everyone had voted and closed the election. There was one poll for the entire county, which the sheriff moved from place to place as he thought best. The franchise was exercised by voice vote, not more than six electors being admitted to the room at one time.[19] Immediately it was clear that the contest would be hard fought. Carleton's assumption that the "violent party spirit" prevailing in the days of Halifax rule was dead proved naive.[20] The rival slates poured propaganda into the press, circulated handbills and tickets listing their names, hired ferries to convey voters across St. John harbour and supplied cheer at tippling houses. The opposition promised "impeachment" of the former agents and directors. The government candidates accused Dickinson's slate of seeking public office for private ends. But soon, what might have been a spirited campaign of brief duration culminating in a triumph for the Lower Cove was transformed into five months of bitter recrimination and cleavage. The watershed event was the Mallard House riot.

Mob action was fairly common in eighteenth-century America, especially around the Guy Fawkes/Pope Day observance of November 5. Already at Annapolis the controversy between Loyalists and their own version of agents and directors had resulted in disorders. Halifax's elections were notoriously violent. Prolonged rioting over land allocation and race had erupted among Loyalist exiles at Shelburne in 1784. Saint John itself was no stranger to small disorders.[21] In comparison with Loyalist Shelburne, the Mallard House riot was no great affair. It was less the event itself than the regime's panicked reaction that turned it into a political parting of the ways.

After Saint John's first day of voting, Sheriff Oliver moved the poll across the harbour to the Carleton neighbourhood. Then on November 9 he adjourned the poll to the Mallard House, headquarters of the Upper Coves. That night at McPherson's tavern in the Lower Cove the crowd was, in Elias Hardy's words, "very drunk."[22] When John Keaquick, an opposition worker, invited an Upper Cove supporter to approach him and receive a caning, a quarrel broke out and the mood became ugly. Eye-witness testimony in the later criminal trial captures some of the outcry:

> Let's go up — they are at Mallards
> Damn 'em — we'll Mob them
> Let's go up — [the Upper Coves] dare not come
> out.

As a mob was forming for the one-third of a mile advance on the Mallard House, Sheriff Oliver failed to quiet them.

Armed with clubs and missiles the crowd — some said forty, others said a hundred — marched to the Upper Cove and surrounded Mallard's. Drinking inside were about thirty supporters of the government candidates. Already there had been rumours that the "Lower Covers were coming to flog 'em." Again Sheriff Oliver commanded peace. An Upper Cover urged Elias Hardy to quiet the crowd. "You are daring us to come on," he answered.

John Jenkins approached the Mallard's door aggressively. "Damn it, I will go in, it is a tavern," he declared. Defenders pummelled him on the steps, and backwards into the crowd he went. James Higgins cried, "By God, we will have that house down before morning," and "Huzza for the Lower Cove." Another urged, "Come on, my boys, we'll soon dislodge 'em."

And so began a general siege of the Mallard House. One onlooker was the king's printer, who gave his version of events:

"The mob, after the most violent threats against those who were in the house, wounding several gentlemen who defended the passage at the door, and in vain endeavouring to force the door, made a general attack upon the house with stones and brick-bats, and soon demolished all the windows. The gentlemen within, fearing immediate destruction to themselves, then returned the stones and brick-bats upon the mob, who began to grow very violent and outrageous. By this means, and the seasonable interposition of troops from Fort Howe, in aid of the exertions of the civil magistrates, the mob was dispersed."[23]

The arrival of soldiers from the 54th Regiment put an end to the attack, though stragglers took their vengeance on the windows of John MacGeorge, one of the Upper Cove candidates. As was usual with mob attacks on buildings, there were no serious injuries. Six opposition supporters were confined to the lock-up at Fort Howe to await trial for riot, and perhaps some others were detained temporarily.[24] Use of troops to quell a riot may seem foreseeable in a town where the governor worried that two companies of soldiers were insufficient to guard the peace and regretted the absence of a prison ship in the harbour. But intervention of the military in civil affairs was a sensitive constitutional issue in eighteenth-century America. It would linger in the memory of many Saint Johners as an ominous government misstep.[25]

The Mallard House riot was the first incident of mob violence since Carleton's arrival. To the ever-watchful American press it was no more than the blackened eyes and bloodied noses typical of urban elections, but to New Brunswick's governing elite it was shocking.[26] Sower's *Royal Gazette* branded it a crime of the "*most* serious complexion." Governor Carleton blamed the opposition candidates for supplying drink to the lowest classes. Abandoning what he saw as a policy of mildness, he now vowed to "hold the Reins of Government with a strait hand" and punish those who did not fall in line.[27] To prevent further violence, the Council instructed Sheriff Oliver to forbid candidates from supplying voters with liquor. He was also to banish from the hustings political flags and badges and threatening or seditious language.[28] Oliver waited for more than a week to resume polling, hoping a reaction would set in against the slate whose supporters had perpetrated this "daring riot." The reopened poll continued daily from noon to 3 p.m. until the marathon election finally concluded on November 24, seventeen days after it had begun.

Voting was open, not secret. Everyone knew daily that the Lower Cove candidates were in the lead, even when polling resumed after the riot. Only desperate measures could save the election for the pro-Carleton ticket. Upper Cove tacticians, including the sheriff, decided that government office holders and the soldiers of the Fort Howe garrison would have to be included in the vote. And so, on the 19th, Oliver permitted a sergeant of the 54th Regiment to vote. Then Oliver himself and three customs men voted, all supporting the government ticket.[29] On the same principle Upper Cove strategists planned on voting a further 160 officers and men of the Fort Howe garrison.[30] Had they succeeded, it would have elected the entire Bliss slate, albeit narrowly.

Two factors prevented the pro-government candidates from winning this way. First, according to William Cobbett, later notorious as a radical journalist in England but in 1785 a corporal at Fort Howe, the soldiers in the garrison favoured the Lower Cove candidates. Despite their role only days earlier in breaking up the Mallard House riot, the rank and file felt solidarity with the Loyalist political dissenters.

Second, for nearly a century there had been a movement in Britain to reduce executive influence in the House of Commons. Legislation barred those in the pay of the Crown — office-holders, contractors, pensioners — from election to the Commons or even voting. Just three years earlier Parliament had disenfranchised revenue officers. Allowing three customs men to vote at Saint John had already distanced New Brunswick from the British model. Opening the polls to 160 Army officers and men would be egregious. There was probably no English or Irish example of common soldiers voting. In Britain this was practically impossible, as ordinary serving men would not have met the property qualification; but in the unique circumstances of New Brunswick in 1785 there was no property bar. All that was required was three months' residence, and the entire Fort Howe garrison had already been made to swear before a notary that they were "inhabitants" who met this qualification.[31]

When the Lower Cove candidates heard of this desperate plan and protested to Carleton, he quietly instructed that the garrison not be voted. Here the governor walked a tricky line, for once clearly independent of his advisors. The garrison strategy would give his supporters the election and must have passed legal muster with candidates Bliss and Chipman, the law officers of the Crown. Yet the governor knew that allowing officers to vote, to say nothing of private soldiers, would be indefensible to his superiors in London and would be a serious constitutional blunder. It would also inflame anti-administration feeling in a community of exiles that had just spent two decades debating constitutional niceties with the Patriots and understood them well. Carleton let it be known that the garrison voting scheme should go no further.

Now that the too-clever plan of voting the military had fallen through, there was no point in protracting the election further. When Sheriff Oliver closed the poll on November 24 his official records showed that neither backlash from the riot nor desperate tactics by government supporters had prevailed.

The margin of opposition victory was impressive, an average of 625 votes to 508.[32]

Lower Covers	*Upper Covers*
Dickinson 650	Bliss 500
Lightfoot 625	Chipman 497
Bonsall 626	Billopp 512
Grim 600	Pagan 509
Boggs 612	Hazard 535
Reid 636	MacGeorge 494

LAWS TORTURED TO THE PURPOSE OF A PARTY

The New Brunswick elite's vision of the most "gentlemanlike" government on earth did not include a political opposition. Theirs was an age in which opposing political alignments were not seen as necessary, permanent or wholly legitimate. If this were so for Britain, then how much more so for a model Loyalist community whose exiled inhabitants had been ruined by too much politics in the old colonies? True, Carleton and his advisors soon became aware that their inherited colony was not a blank political slate and that a "violent party spirit" had prevailed in the days of rule from Halifax. Yet they assumed that all tears were wiped away now that the king's governor was on the spot. A formerly aggrieved and agitated multitude had become, in Ward Chipman's expression, the "fortunate ones." Aided by the royal bounty, they had raised an already flourishing colony. Their proper attitude towards the king's local representatives was grateful obedience. Certainly, New Brunswick's rulers were not to be opposed.

So it was that, despite Saint John's difficult birth, Carleton could assume in calling his election that political dissent was entirely done away. When the campaign produced first a riot and then victory for the faction whose supporters had caused it, the governor and his Council viewed the scene with "utter astonishment."[33] At the very outset of their Loyalist experiment the goal of a model colonial constitution was in peril. Seven bold critics led by the irrepressible Elias Hardy were set on making their life difficult in the House of Assembly. Victory for the Lower Cove candidates meant their dream of a most gentlemanlike colony had failed when it had hardly begun.

What was to be done? Carleton and his Council might have chosen to respond to the triumph of the Dickinson slate in political terms. They might have used their hoped-for assembly majority to outvote the Lower Covers, or the seductions of patronage to divide them or the passage of time to neutralize them. They might even have agreed to investigate the conduct of the former agents and directors. They chose otherwise. Rather than meet the challenge of political dissent in political terms, they moved to expel their opponents from the political realm altogether. In the days and months following the initial election result they denied the Lower Cove candidates their seats in the House of Assembly, intimidated their lieutenants and muzzled their rank and file. Ultimately they sought to freeze their enemies out of the realm of legitimate political debate by branding them with the high Loyalist crime of disloyalty.

Sheriffs of the eight counties were supposed to respond to Carleton's writs of election by November 24, the day the Saint John poll finally closed. Sheriff Oliver merely sent in a letter. It reported that Attorney-General Bliss and his Upper Cove colleagues had demanded a scrutiny of the votes won by the Lower Cove candidates.[34] The basis of their protest was a list of between two and three hundred votes alleged as ineligible for failure to meet the three-month residency requirement.[35] By this route the government candidates and the compliant Oliver hoped yet to fill Saint John's seats in the House of Assembly with six regime supporters.

The scrutiny would begin just two weeks before the General Assembly itself was to convene. Rather than participate, the Lower Cove candidates appealed to the provincial Council to forbid it. They complained that it would be conducted by a sheriff who had declared openly that "they could not expect any thing else at his Hands but to be their bitter Enemy." Oliver's bias was part of a larger concern that had surfaced already in the threat to allow the revenue officers and the garrison to vote: whether the election would abide by English laws and practices or whether the sheriff was free to adopt any procedure that would succeed in electing the pro-government candidates. Technically, English laws did not apply, and of course New Brunswick had no election statute of its own. At the outset, the Council had decreed simply that the franchise would be open to white adult males resident in their county for three months. But when Oliver allowed the customs men to vote and showed that he was prepared to accommodate the soldiers, he provoked a furious argument from the Lower Cove candidates over what election laws the sheriff should observe. "You will remember, Sir," they chided him later, "that the Statute Law of England relative to Elections was repeatedly urged by us and as often rejected as not extending hither and with it of course the Bill of Rights, which is an English Statute and the basis of Parliamentary Freedom."

But now that the government candidates had been outpolled, and Oliver saw advantage in holding a scrutiny, he was willing to embrace British practice, particularly a notorious election scrutiny that had just concluded. Yet no sooner did he profess to take this scrutiny as his model than he deviated from it crucially: he would judge the votes personally rather than turn the matter over to a less engaged party, and he would begin by considering all of the complaints from the government slate before taking up any objections that the opposition might lodge. To the Lower Cove candidates Oliver's repeated manipulation of the law and the Council's refusal to overrule him signified that they would be "robbed" of their rights.[36] Unwilling to see "Laws ... tortured to the purpose of a party and the freedom of Elections denied," they decided, unwisely, to boycott Oliver's "Pretended scrutiny."[37]

Beginning just before Christmas the sheriff and the government slate of candidates went through the motions of a scrutiny lasting four hours daily for five days. The candidates objected to, and Oliver disallowed, nearly two hundred opposition votes, sufficient to reverse the polling result and give victory to the attorney-general's slate by a comfortable margin. Even so, as the king's printer gloated in a witty theological pun, the Upper Covers "had objected to many more voters, which were not scrutinized, as those already condemned, were deemed sufficient to *make their election sure*."[38] Here are the new (and old) standings:

Lower Covers	Upper Covers
	(all unchanged)
Dickinson 468 (650)	Bliss 500
Lightfoot 444 (625)	Chipman 497
Bonsall 445 (626)	Billopp 512
Grim 418 (600)	Pagan 509
Boggs 434 (612)	Hazard 535
Reid 456 (636)	MacGeorge 494

Now, a month late, Sheriff Oliver made his formal return to the writ of election, filling Saint John's seats in the House of Assembly with the six government candidates.[39]

What was the opposition slate to do? In the long run they might appeal to the British government — a doubtful proposition.[40] In the short term their tactic was to keep the issue alive by laying their case before the new House of Assembly. As Chipman reported to Edward Winslow, "Owing to the stupidity of the Lower Cove Candidates in not attending the scrutiny and defending their votes the Sheriff has returned us, but our seats are to be contested by vehement petition."[41]

THE ODIOUS AND DETESTABLE APPELLATION OF REBELS

Six days from the close of the Saint John election scrutiny, Governor Carleton seated himself in the chair of state in the makeshift Council chamber to open the first session of New Brunswick's General Assembly. As a wordsmith Thomas Carleton was no Thomas Jefferson. The British government's "parental care" had rescued Loyalists from persecution at the end of the American war. Now its "peculiar munificence" was supplying their wants in the resettlement process. The new United States might take life, liberty and pursuit of happiness as public values but Carleton urged New Brunswickers to embrace "sobriety, industry and the practice of religion." In his sole nod to posterity, he declared the new colony an "asylum of loyalty" that could not fail of becoming the flourishing "envy" of the republic to the south. It could not fail, that is, as long as "all party distinctions amongst us" were suppressed.[42]

In an irony no one could miss, Carleton had brought together the appointed Council (upper house) and the elected House of Assembly at Thomas Mallard's tavern. Evidently its windows, demolished by riot two months earlier, were back in repair, and perhaps the lingering smell of beer was meant to speed the provincial fathers at their thirsty work. A busy lot they were. That first legislative session took up seventy-five bills and turned out 130 large printed pages of statutes. But before any laws were made there was the matter of whether the six members for the City and County of Saint John were lawfully elected. Lower Covers sent in four petitions against seating the pro-government candidates. All focussed on the conduct of Sheriff Oliver. Two arrived from Lower Cove supporters whose votes were disallowed in the scrutiny. This, they said, had robbed them of their rights and injured them greatly in reputation. Another petition came in from two hundred opposition voters. It was the Lower Cove candidates themselves who had most to say. They cited two election tactics used against them as especially offensive. Their supporters had been threatened with denial of the royal bounty of provisions.[43] Most chilling, several of the candidates and their supporters had been "branded with the odious and detestable appellation of Rebels."

Two weeks later the petition from the Lower Cove candidates was examined minutely, with many witnesses called by lawyers on both sides.[44] Then legal counsel debated the question of whether the Dickinson slate's decision to boycott the scrutiny prevented them from contesting its result. On this issue the House decided, in an unrecorded vote, that the Lower Covers had indeed lost the right to contend that the judgements made at the scrutiny were wrong.

Then proceedings turned to the complaints against Sanford Oliver. After further speeches from the lawyers and some debate, the house resolved that the fiercely biased sheriff had acted "legally, fairly and with impartiality." The division on this whitewash was ten to four, with Elias Hardy (as legal counsel to the Lower Covers) and the six Upper Covers whose seats were being contested, abstaining. The house dismissed the other three petitions without discussion.

To many opposition supporters this result was devastating psychologically as well as politically. Their election victory had been stolen. The partisan conduct of the sheriff had been upheld. The record of the former agents and directors had escaped scrutiny and censure once again. Was this the British liberty for which they had resisted revolution? Had their promised land of loyalty become another Egyptian bondage? Was this to be the constitution of the most gentlemanlike government on earth? We see the blind frustration in tavern talk overheard by the toadying king's printer on the evening of Sheriff Oliver's exoneration.

"Sitting in Mr [Charles] McPherson's Coffee Room ... Mr [George] Handiside [sic] came in and after speaking to Mr [William] Lewis [the printer] he pointed at a List of Names posted up in the said Room, which were objected to as bad Votes on the Scrutiny and ... expressed himself to this effect, that the House of Assembly *ought to be tore limb from limb* — upon which I took him up ... He damn'd me ... [H]e finally denied having said they *ought* to be torn limb from limb but ... *he wondered the People did not tear them limb from limb.*"[45]

Christopher Sower reported these inflammatory words to the speaker of the house, who issued a speaker's warrant for Handesyde's arrest. Accused before the House of Assembly on January 26 of uttering "certain opprobrious Words in Contempt and Breach of the privileges of this House and tending to excite Sedition," he was voted guilty. His punishment was to remain in irons until he begged the house's pardon on his knees. Handesyde, known thereafter as the "kneeling man," complied.[46]

The intemperate George Handesyde probably spoke for many. As his little drama played out in the House of Assembly, 449 opposition supporters reaffirmed solidarity through the device of an elaborate address of welcome to Fort Howe's new commissary, Samuel Hake. A well-connected though shifty Loyalist, Hake had served with Hardy and Tertullus Dickinson in August 1783 on the committee that prepared the counter-petition to the Fifty-Five at New York. Evacuated to London, he had co-authored pamphlets defending Governor Parr against propaganda attacks by the Fifty-Five and so had worked indirectly against Nova Scotia partition. The hundreds who signed the address welcoming Hake did so as a gesture of renewed defiance against those who had just triumphed in the house.[47]

The most vivid evidence of frustration among the dissidents following the house's whitewash of Oliver takes the

form of two public protests. Each triggered a criminal prosecution for sedition — incitement to rebellion. One was a
letter from *Americanus* published in Lewis and Ryan's *Saint
John Gazette* of February 22. As with most statements of
Loyalist grievance, it begins by invoking the sufferings of the
revolution and the shock of arriving at the St. John River to
an unsurveyed wilderness. It catalogues the old grievances
against the agents and directors and plays on the emotive
suggestion that the Loyalist elite had a plan to reduce the
rank and file of exiles to the level of tenant farmers ("slaves").
Having recited these "multiplied grievances," *Americanus*
concluded with the language of outrage:

"[W]e are distressed in looking forward. We scarcely
dare view tomorrow. Our Provisions almost gone. Our
lands not brought into cultivation. Our Loyalty suspected
… [T]ear the Mask from their faces, and exhibit their naked
Enormities to the whole World … [L]et us not disgrace
Loyalty with Cowardice. My distressed Countrymen, let us
oppose every the least Violation of our Privileges, for the
Preservation of which we have sacrificed our all. Submit not
to petit Tyrants."

Publication of these inflammatory words at the height of
unrest over the assembly's seating of the pro-government
candidates led to the arrest of Lewis and Ryan for publishing a scandalous and seditious libel. The actual writer of the
piece was never known but that was unimportant. What was
critical was using the affair to neutralize the troublesome
printers, either through intimidation or financial ruin. The
agents and directors had failed at this in the *Soldier* affair
of two years earlier. Now Carleton's regime was successful. Within two weeks, and well before their criminal trial,

Lewis and Ryan dissolved their partnership and the *Saint John Gazette* ceased publication. "The Printers have laid aside their paper," the governor chortled, "and the Citizens disown these incendiaries."[48] Carleton's political enemies had lost their access to the press.

By the time *Americanus*'s letter appeared, dissidents at Saint John and settlements upriver as far as Fredericton were putting their signatures to another vehement protest. It was a petition to the governor and became the final and most objectionable expression of popular opposition to his regime. Drawn up at the Lower Cove just after the assembly's decision to seat the six government candidates, it reflects intense disorientation and despair. By February 5, Lower Cove agents were circulating a copy in interior Sunbury County. Two weeks later Oliver Bourdett and a bowed but unrepentant George Handesyde (the "kneeling man") offered it for signature in York County. In a region settled entirely by disbanded soldiers and their pro-government officers, this was a bold canvass, and it was only with some firmness that Edward Winslow prevented the young "bucks" of his neighbourhood from seizing and expelling them. However, in his capacity as a justice of the peace, Winslow did publish a notice against Bourdett and Handesyde, labelling them "vagrants" who were spreading "an inflammatory and seditious libel against the lawful authority of this province."[49] If they reappeared, Winslow would put them in the stocks.

No copy of the Sunbury petition survives, and there is no indication of how many signatures it attracted. Upwards of three hundred signed the version circulated at Saint John. In it they called themselves Loyalists and local electors, so all had presumably voted for the Dickinson slate of candidates. The fact that hundreds were still willing to align themselves publicly with the dissidents in the face of government intimidation reflects their naive faith in the idea of British liberty. Rather than allowing the petition campaign to run its course and ignoring it, the governing elite pounced on the occasion to send one more signal that opposition to their regime was illegitimate. That message took the form of a new law against public petitioning. Petitioning was a ritual of political expression that carried considerable freight in English constitutional history, and the same was true in the old colonies.[50] In resurrecting from the reign of Charles II a law against political petitioning, the governing elite sent a fierce warning to its detractors. They did so in defiance of the English *Bill of Rights* declaration that it was the "right of the subjects to petition the king, and all commitments and prosecutions for such petitioning are illegal."

It was the Council, acting in its legislative capacity, that initiated the bill and sent it down to the House of Assembly. Chief Justice Ludlow himself introduced it.[51] Entitled an *Act against Tumults and Disorders, upon pretence of preparing or presenting Public Petitions, or other Addresses, to the Governor, or General Assembly*, its declared purpose was:

> To prevent tumultuous and other disorderly soliciting, and procuring of Hands, by private persons, to Petitions, Complaints, Remonstrances, and Declarations, and other Addresses, to the Governor, Council and Assembly, or any or either of them for alteration of matters established by Law, redress of pretended grievances in Church or

State, or other public concernments, being made
use of to serve the ends of factious and seditious
persons, to the violation of the Public peace.

Its effect was to criminalize solicitation of more than
twenty signatures to petitions for redress of "pretended"
grievances in church or state without the prior consent of
three county justices of the peace or the grand jury.

If the language and the timing of the *Tumultuous Petitioning
Act* were intimidating, so was the penalty for violation — a
fine of one hundred pounds and three months' imprisonment.
But the act had a broader significance. In the eighteenth
century many folk did not read and could not vote and so
were excluded from participation in the political community. Petitioning was one of the recognized public forms or
rituals by which politically speechless men and women could
nevertheless make their voices heard. When Carleton and
his advisors followed up their success in excluding the Lower
Cove candidates and silencing the *Saint John Gazette* with a
law effectively banning petitioning, they removed the only
remaining means of lawful political expression for many
among the rank and file of dissenters. Their object was not
to stifle one petition but to stifle dissent.

The House of Assembly passed the *Tumultuous Petitioning
Act* on March 1. The vote was ten to four, with Elias Hardy
opposed.[52] The following day Carleton gave royal assent.
Undeterred by the new law passed for the very purpose of
obstructing their petition, on March 6 its authors — Claudius
Charles, William Thompson, Joseph Montgomery and John
Carnes — called on the provincial secretary to present it.
Jonathan Odell turned them away but told the four that they

might hand it to Governor Carleton personally the next day. He also warned that the law to suppress such petitions was now in effect. The presenters could hardly have been unaware of the law, so Odell's warning was part of the choreography of confrontation. At the appointed time the four waited on the governor and presented a version with 330 signatures. For doing so they were seized, examined before Mayor Ludlow, charged with circulating a seditious libel and jailed.[53] They remained in prison for two months until trial. Chief Justice Ludlow, author of the *Tumultuous Petitioning Act*, refused even to hear a *habeas corpus* application to free them in the interim on bail.[54]

Among the many political compositions surviving from Loyalist Saint John, the petition of March 1786 is uniquely compelling. Its very lack of polish gives it a heartfelt eloquence, as in its sonorous opening sentence.

> We His Majesty's dutiful and affectionate Subjects,
> Electors of the City & County of Saint John,
> after having suffered every Evil, which could be
> inflicted upon loyal Subjects, by the cruel Hand of
> Usurpation, for an Adherence to the Person of our
> King and His Government, and a most oppressive
> Tyranny since our Arrival in this Place, patiently
> have borne those Hardships from a due Regard to
> the British Constitution, under the firm Persuasion
> of being relieved from our Bondage upon Your
> Excellency's arrival, cannot now sit Silent under the
> complicated Grievances we suffer and the fearful
> Apprehension of what this infant Settlement must
> undergo, if such dangerous Measures are persisted

in, which threaten no less than a speedy Dissolution
of the same or a Revolution to us no less dreadful,
particularly the most daring, violent and alarming
Invasion of our Liberties striking directly at the
Vitals of our most excellent Constitution.

These sensational references to "oppressive Tyranny,"
"Bondage" and "complicated Grievances," and the suggestion of a possible mass return to the United States or a
"Revolution" were alone enough to invite prosecution. But
there was more. After a catalogue of election grievances and
a request that Carleton call a fresh vote, the petitioners made
a threat no government could ignore. They asserted that
laws made by an assembly "so unconstitutionally composed"
had no binding force. This was a deliberate confrontation
with authority. It cannot be wondered that the four presenters were arrested on a warrant alleging they had published an
inflammatory libel which "denieth the authority of the Laws
... and the legality of the Assembly now sitting" and tending
to incite rebellion.[55]

At no time in the record of early Saint John does the question of what it meant to be a Loyalist come more sharply into
focus than during this petition episode. Its 330 signatories
identified themselves repeatedly in terms of their loyalty.
The saw it as their prime characteristic, and the language
of the petition expresses this poignantly. Yet on the basis
of the same document, Carleton's regime prosecuted the
four presenters for attempting "to alienate and withdraw
the Affection, Fidelity, and Allegiance of his ... Majesty's
Subjects ... from his said Majesty." But rebels against the
king do not exchange a successful revolution for exile in a

wilderness. Saint John's dissidents were asserting loyalty to the king while reserving their right to resist "Subversi[on] of the first Priviledges of the British Constitution" by the king's local representative. Carleton and his circle responded with just the reverse: opposition to governor and Council was tantamount to opposition to the king. In the excited imagination of Attorney-General Bliss, circulating this "most seditious" petition was "little short of an overt act of High Treason."[56]

The petition's language, sponsorship and signatures are revealing in a second way. They indicate that the former leaders of dissent at Saint John — Hardy and Dickinson — had retired from the cause after their defeat in the House of Assembly.[57] They did not draw up the petition, for it lacks the literary flourish of other Lower Cove efforts. They did not even sign it. Hardy's circle would not have been so foolish as to attack the authority of the legislature or to present such a document to the governor in deliberate violation of the new law. They would have known that such actions played into the government's hands, lending a retrospective legitimacy to the whole campaign of repression since the riot. But a number of second-rank leaders in the Lower Cove faction and more than three hundred followers were so frustrated by the course of events since the unhappy day they landed at Saint John that they would say and do what wiser heads would not.

The six Mallard House rioters, printers Lewis and Ryan and the four presenters of the seditious election petition came to trial at the May 1786 session of the Supreme Court. In light of the regime's mixed results in these prosecutions, the procedural background to the trials is worth examining.

Normal criminal procedure was to take prisoners before the county grand jury to decide whether there was enough evidence to put them on trial. In the case of the rioters it is uncertain whether this procedure was followed. In the case of the two sedition prosecutions it was not. Attorney-General Bliss chose to lay informations against Lewis and Ryan and the four presenters directly in the Supreme Court, something only an attorney general could do. His motive is obvious. The governing circle, especially one in which both law officers were from Massachusetts, had reason to fear that no American grand jury would charge defendants with seditious libel.[58] There had not been a successful prosecution for decades. But once Attorney General Bliss actually brought the case to trial, as he was entitled to do by virtue of his office, the trial jury offered no such problem of control. At a trial for seditious libel the jury could decide only the question of whether the defendants had "published." It was the role of the judge to decide whether that publication was seditious, and in New Brunswick all judges were members of the governor's Council.

How convenient. The verdict against Lewis, Ryan and the four petition presenters, when prosecuted and tried under such an arrangement, was a foregone conclusion. They were duly convicted and fined.

In the case of those charged with the Mallard House riot there was no similar way to control the trial jury, which had complete jurisdiction over the question of guilt. This may explain why only three of the six rioters brought to trial were convicted.[59] It also explains a curious sidelight to the case of the four presenters. As the *Tumultuous Petitioning Act* had been passed for the very purpose of suppressing their petition, and as Jonathan Odell had threatened them expressly with prosecution under the legislation, why were they not charged under that law but rather with the common-law crime of sedition? The answer must be that the government mistrusted the jury to convict under the statute, opting instead for the procedural advantage given the prosecution when the charge was seditious libel.

These three trials in May 1786 mark the denouement of the campaign against political dissent in early Saint John. Within a week of their close, Carleton was reporting complacently to London that his policy of governing with a "strait" hand had met with "every success." He had brought the province into "perfect order and obedience." His opposition had "failed" — he did not explain how — to win seats in the assembly. Following this failure they had "procured by every Artifice libellous petitions and published inflammatory pieces in a Newspaper." Blandly, he continued: "A prosecution has been carried on in the Supreme Court against the Promoters of these disorders ... The Rioters, Printers, and those who presented the Petition have been severally convicted and punished and I can venture to assure your Lordship that faction is at an end here."[60] Carleton boasted that his campaign to make the Loyalist colony passive and obedient was an entire success.

CHAPTER 5
PERFECT TRANQUILITY

The May 1786 criminal trials of the two printers, the four petition presenters and six of the Mallard House rioters were the climactic scene of Saint John's turbulent political birth. But a final question remains. What made the public life of Loyalist Saint John so remarkable, in ways never seen in eastern Canada again?

In a settlement of about three thousand people why were there *two* newspapers? How could David Melville think of putting out a three hundred-page history of the place just sixteen months from its founding? Why were press columns filled with political contributions from writers calling themselves *Horatio, Claudius, Plain Dealer, Urbanitatis, A Citizen, A Native American Loyalist, A British Subject* and so on in a setting so small that concealing one's identity was nearly impossible? What was the point of publishing dozens of learned, witty, intense election screeds in a place where the twelve candidates might have canvassed every voter personally? Why was public life in early Saint John so remarkably literary when we know, from the very scale of the place, that its effective political culture must have been oral?

The broad answer is that the Saint John of the 1780s was not special. True, Saint John dominated a whole colony in a way that the far larger Loyalist town of Shelburne in Nova Scotia did not. But Saint John's political character was not very different from that of pre-evacuation New York City, or the Nova Scotian centres of Loyalist resettlement, or among the loyal exiles at Sorel or Cornwall. Loyalists entered their exile not as future Canadians but as colonial Americans set down in a wilderness. Saint John's notably literary warfare echoes the political ways of pre-revolutionary New York, Philadelphia and Boston. That is why the story of early Saint John holds as much interest for students of the United States as for their Canadian counterparts.

IS THE ENSLAVING OF US AN OBJECT THEY WANT?

In making their case at the 1785 election, Lower Covers renewed the cry for what they called impeachment and prosecution of Saint John's former agents and directors.[1] Although agent misdeeds were long in the past, their memory lingered as an emotive symbol of official betrayal. The opposition also resurrected for the campaign the old outcry against the Fifty-Five, that group of self-important Loyalists exposed in attempting a Nova Scotian land grab in 1783. Two of six government election candidates, Ward Chipman and Christopher Billopp, had belonged to that much-abused number. They became a useful propaganda link between the old resistance to the Fifty-Five and the new resistance to New Brunswick's governing elite.[2] Both ideas came together when an opposition writer warned Saint John voters not to "blow up the Constitution" on November 7 (the first day of voting, just after Guy Fawkes night) by electing "agents, agentees [and] fifty-fivers."[3]

There were three issues in particular that sustained the opposition's election case.

THE SECTION ISSUE

"I hope in time," wrote Governor Parr in 1784, that Loyalist exiles will "be brought to think they are one and the same people, in which light the four Northern Colonies have never look'd upon those to the Southward, and from this cause arises a great part of their animosity."[4] Parr was stating a truism. Colonial Americans were intensely local. Each ethnic group and each colony had its distinctive character, local pride and special jealousies. New England, especially Massachusetts, imagined itself foremost among the mainland British provinces and was resented by the others.[5] So it was that the colonies in rebellion saw themselves as thirteen allied republics, not yet as united states.

This American tendency to view the world in sectional terms pervaded the Loyalist community, as Parr rightly complained. It was true of the exiles gathered at pre-evacuation New York City where, in dividing up various forms of public assistance or appointment, it was routine to classify Loyalists according to their former colonial home. It was true of refugees in London, where New Englanders drank at one coffee house, New Yorkers at another. And it was true at St. John River. To a writer in the Saint John press, it was simply a fact that Loyalists saw themselves as "British Americans, Scotch Americans, Irish Americans, Dutch

Americans, and native Americans; the last is also subject to thirteen subdivisions, all having local and national attachments." This was human nature. What the writer deplored was the opposition's attempt to turn these benign partialities into prejudices and hates. Lower Covers, he complained, appealed for votes on sectional lines. In particular, they played to a traditional anti–New England — specifically anti-Massachusetts — prejudice.[6]

Saint John had many New Englanders, but most were from Connecticut.[7] The appeal to anti–New England sentiment focused on the exiles from Massachusetts, who numbered perhaps 5 per cent of the total. Although not numerous, they occupied the lion's share of prominent offices: Commissary Tyng, magistrates Leonard and Coffin, Attorney General Bliss, Solicitor General Chipman, Surrogate General Winslow, judges Putnam and Upham, Sheriff Oliver. And they knew it. To a fellow Massachusetts Loyalist, Attorney General Bliss cursed his election opponents for thinking themselves "entitled ... to rule over Yankees, as over Negroes." Earlier, this obvious concentration of power had led those opposing separation from Nova Scotia to ask, "how many gentlemen from the province of Massachusetts do you suppose will be without lucrative appointments?" in the event of partition. Their agility at rising to the top showed that some had "followed the fortune of our King, as numbers followed our Saviour — for the loaves and fishes." With two Massachusetts lawyers at the head of the Upper Cove election ticket it was inevitable that sectional jealousy would become part of the political maneuvering. When one dissident decried a regime in which "New-England-men" were in charge of public affairs, he referred pointedly to those from the "meridian of Boston." Magistrate George Leonard was denounced not by name but as the *Miller of Boston.* Even Massachusetts's Puritan heritage did not escape mockery. In scrambling to reestablish themselves in a world of exile, Loyalists from the Bay colony acted with "superior *cunning*," being "*great sticklers for the doctrine of saving grace.*"[8]

CONSTITUTIONAL ISSUES

Americans of the revolutionary generation were acutely sensitive to constitutional matters and understood several of Saint John's election issues in constitutional terms. None was of a fundamental nature. In contrast to debates preceding the Revolution, none generated more than a passing invocation of John Locke, Cesare Beccaria and other theorists. Yet constitutional debate among Saint John's Loyalists played a significant role in the crisis. One aspect was occasional protests against "taxation" without representation, a melodramatic reference to a charge of two shillings to participate in the lottery for town lots at Parr-town and Carleton. More serious was the anger aroused by Carleton's use of soldiers to suppress the Mallard House riot and then patrol the streets. In seventeenth-century England, formation of a "standing" army had been a great grievance against the Stuart monarchs. It was eventually prohibited by the *Bill of Rights*, though nearly annual *Mutiny Act*s allowed the Crown to maintain an army for the time being. Ever since the peace of 1763 Americans had fretted over the continuing presence of British garrisons along their Atlantic coast, notably at Halifax. They felt that this standing army in their midst was unconstitutional, a feeling that helped poison the public mind against the idea of empire. In the military reality of the

1780s no one could have objected to the garrisoning of Fort Howe — near the Saint John settlement rather than in it. But as Americans, Loyalists instinctively saw use of the military in matters normally reserved for civil authority as alarming, especially in a settlement where there seemed a whole constellation of threats to liberty. This explains the indignation in the seditious 1786 election petition at the regime's "unlawful" use of Fort Howe soldiers in civilian affairs:

> [W]e have publicly seen British Subjects confined
> in Irons, Carried into a Garrison and there
> examined under the authority of a military Guard
> and Prosecutions still hanging over their Heads for
> supposed Offences.
>   One of our legal Representatives confined in a
> Sentry Box at the discretion and by the Order of a
> Private Soldier.
>   The Military introduced and unnecessarily
> and unlawfully patrolling the streets, during an
> Election, to the Terror and Alarm of the peaceable
> inofensive Inhabitants.

The most sustained constitutional issue that Lower Covers put in play was the propriety of government officers (Bliss and Chipman) seeking places in the elective House of Assembly.[9] Elias Hardy wrote at length in the *Saint John Gazette* against electing men "in the service of government." His rationale was that introducing members of the executive into the legislative branch would unbalance the division of constitutional responsibilities dangerously. From history he argued that it was unusual to elect the attorney or solicitor general in Pennsylvania or New York, and he instanced the exclusion of Nova Scotia's attorney general from that colony's lower house.[10] Other propagandists linked opposition to Bliss and Chipman as Crown lawyers to hostility towards lawyers generally.[11] Hardy, himself a lawyer, confessed that most lawyers "are more disposed to argue than to deliberate, and frequently do as much hurt in public assemblies as they do good." Anti-lawyer sentiment was sufficiently potent that Attorney General Bliss named it publicly, criticizing opposition candidates for *not* being lawyers and thereby ill-acquainted with the science of legislation. He noted that Crown law officers were almost invariably elected as Members of Parliament in England and most of the former colonies. As for Nova Scotia, Loyalists should not heed precedents from that notoriously republican province. If Nova Scotia's attorney general were unelectable it was because he was "too much a *Government man*" to win favour with the mob.

"SLAVERY"

When Lower Covers charged that the local elite were designing to reduce the majority of Loyalists to the status of "slaves," they invoked an argument with dreadful associations. Among the generation preceding the Loyalist exodus, no argument was heard more frequently than that Parliament had a deep-laid plot to reduce American colonists to the status of slaves. Viewing the American controversy through this lens, Patriots had cast Parliament in the role of aggressor and themselves as waging a conservative resistance. Defeat in this campaign against their birthright of liberty would be tantamount to slavery.

In one of the earliest instances of the land grievance becoming a political issue, the *Spectator* poet had likened the relationship of Saint Johners and their agents to that of ancient Israelites enslaved to Pharaoh. The agents' "main design," he charged, was to render the rank and file of Loyalists "like slaves." Two years later the seditious *Americanus* conjured with the same theme when he demanded bitterly, "Is the enslaving of us an Object they want?"[12] Loyalists inhabited a world in which slavery had a vivid practical meaning. Stanton Hazard, the most popular of the Upper Cove election candidates, was a Rhode Island slave trader. Many blacks at Saint John were slaves. One of the earliest issues of the *Saint John Gazette* prints a lengthy advertisement for recapture of six slaves escaped from a single master.[13] Most free blacks had been slaves until recently.

But when dissidents spoke of slavery they did not mean a literal loss of personal freedom. They meant reduction to the status of tenant farmers. As early as the great counter-petition at New York in August 1783, the rank and file of Loyalists cried alarm that the Fifty-Five were designing to "enslave" ordinary Refugees by making them "submit to be Tenants" on great Nova Scotia estates. On the same theme Samuel Hake accused the Fifty-Five of having a "plan of making tenants of their suffering brethren"; he likened them to "syndics" looking for "vassals" and to the "Patroons" of New Netherland, whose feudal manors along the Hudson River had become part of New York in 1664. Nathaniel Horton's Refugee company concluded its October 1783 statement of grievances with the fear that the land-granting process would be manipulated to make them tenants, depriving them of the franchise and other civic rights enjoyed by freeholders. A little later the seditious *Soldier* feared that his fellow exiles would have to become "tenants to a fortunate few." Signers of the great seditious election petition of 1786 complained of their "bondage."[14]

As Hake's language suggests, this slavery/tenancy theme had a special resonance for the sort of Loyalist gathered at Saint John. The greatest number was from the colony of New York, and nearly all the others had passed some years on the lower Hudson during the war. Much of New York's rural population were tenant farmers on Hudson Valley manors. Conditions of tenancy varied greatly. Many tenants had almost the same status as freeholders. But whether benign or oppressive, the idea of creating Old World-style manors on a continent where all adult white males thought themselves entitled to be freeholders was offensive. The resultant landlord-tenant tension was a constant in New York's rough political life. The gentlemanlike vision that gave rise to Hudson Valley manors was not confined to New York. The largely empty pre-Loyalist townships along the St. John River and on neighbouring St. John's (Prince Edward) Island reflected the same feudal impulse. When Saint John Loyalists cautioned each other against supporting the local elite lest it lead to the slavery of tenancy, they invoked a living part of their collective experience.

GIDDY FACTION CANNOT HERE BE STILL

The main anxiety of Governor Carleton and his Council was public order. They aimed to give New Brunswick a "firm & orderly Government." Their object was to instill "habits of decorum and industry," to promote "sobriety, industry and the practice of Religion," to reinforce the "ideal of military subordination," to "reclaim the multitude" to a "perfect order and obedience."[15] They had a corresponding horror of a society in which order was lacking. As they felt the heat of opposition to their policies, words like disorder, tumult, confusion, irregularity, licentiousness and sedition flowed from their pens. By an orderly society the Loyalist elite meant more than an absence of violence in the public roadways. They aimed to create a decorous community in which public affairs were shaped by those whom the Anglican god had been pleased to call to the rank of gentlemen. Their ideal, "gentlemanlike" society comprised "Rulers" (Carleton's term) and "common people" (Winslow's term).

The social earthquake of rebellion, civil war and exile put this hierarchical dream in peril. The position of members of the colonial elite had become precarious. They faced social dislocation and financial ruin. Guy Carleton acknowledged this when he advised Parr that officers in the disbanding Provincial corps were of the "first families" in the colonies, men "born to the fairest possessions"; they should now be "distinguished beyond the ordinary" in land grants.[16] The same assumption underlay the petition of the Fifty-Five. So, too, Edward Winslow viewed his circle of friends as comprising "Gentlemen of the best education — formerly of the first fortunes in the Country."[17] Conversely, in the upheavals of war and exile some ordinary colonials had profited from disorder and aspired above their rightful social station. As fleet after fleet of exiles landed at St. John harbour, more than one observer sensed the uncouth novelty as "gentlemen, merchants, mechanicks, farmers and soldiers mingled in the same crowd; many were struting about in gold and scarlet, while others appeared in the battered garments of

144 LOYALIST REBELLION IN NEW BRUNSWICK

indigence and wo." In a world now turned upside-down, some were "tolerable Wealthy, Some … has seen beter days but is now Reduced to Indigent Circumstances — Numbers Never Saw Such Good days."[18]

Among those who never saw such good days were, or hoped to be, the David Melvilles, Peter Grims and Oliver Bourdetts of the Hardy faction. Recall George Leonard's dismay at the "strange and indelicate" way that he and other gentlemen had been summoned before Chief Justice Finucane in 1784 to answer charges inspired by their social inferiors. "For God's sake," he had urged Edward Winslow, "let us have in our new-expected Province a Chief Justice that will not give credit to every idle report from Barbers and Grog shops." Soon after, the agents and directors were explaining to Governor Parr that the Hardy faction were "men of low birth" whose "present occupations and characters render them unfit for any but the lowest offices in the state." In contrast, they were themselves "gentlemen and men of honour."[19] The agents and directors had failed to keep the low-born in their place, but Thomas Carleton's regime had far greater resources.

THE PATRIOTIC ISSUE

In one of their election handbills the six Upper Cove candidates advertised themselves as "the disinterested Patriot Candidates." In the eighteenth-century world the term "patriot" was a powerful one. It described those who put public good above private advantage — those who were disinterested of every selfish impulse. Thus, those who promoted the candidacy of Stanton Hazard emphasized that they did so "from a Regard to the Public Welfare, totally divested of any interested Motive." To underline the fact that

their own candidacy was influenced by the "most honourable motives, without any selfish views, or considerations
of private interest," the Upper Covers announced that they
would serve in the assembly without pay.[20]

When the government ticket labelled themselves as
"Patriot Candidates" they insinuated that this was not so
of their opponents. They dismissed the Lower Covers as
a "faction." The factious were those who played a political
game. Their object was personal advantage rather than the
public good. The factious were plotters, a party, a cabal. They
were interested, scheming, designing. They were everything
that disinterested patriots were not. "Factious" and similar
adjectives ("artful designing men," "noisy faction," "artful
ambitious men," "boundless ambition") were favourite insults
hurled at Elias Hardy and his Huggeford connections, first
by Parr (before he embraced them), then by the agents and
directors, then by Carleton's administration. At the beginning of his Saint John career Hardy had been merely a
"troublesome fellow." Now he was a designing manipulator,
working for his own "artful purposes."[21]

> "*Suppose, Sir,*" demanded a government
> supporter, "*that while we are exerting ourselves
> in this country to keep the Attorney and Solicitor
> General out of the Assembly, some one gentleman
> [Hardy] of the same learned profession, (who like
> a prophet is despised in his own country) should
> contrive to be returned for a remote part of the
> province [Northumberland County], where his
> name is hardly known: If such a person possessed
> art with evil designs, might he not make a property*

of our middling members [i.e., the Lower Cove
candidates, if elected], and use them as instruments
of faction?"

Another friend of the administration cast Hardy's role in
promoting factious opposition in terms of an Aesopian
fable. An elegantly dressed ape (Hardy) landed on an island
inhabited by weasels (Lower Covers).[22]

> *"It happened that the Weazels were, at that*
> *time, forming a project to sap the foundation of*
> *the government which was in the hands of an*
> *Elephant [Carleton] of great experience and try'd*
> *firmness ... It instantly occurred to them that*
> *he was providentially sent to assist them in their*
> *operations against the Elephant...*

But in planning their coup the weasels discovered that the
ape had once been a lowly weasel himself.

> *The Weazels finding that they had committed*
> *an error, treated the unfortunate Ape with great*
> *contempt, and he was obliged to embrace the*
> *earliest opportunity to abandon the island."*

Moral: Avoid bad company.

Complementing this view of Elias Hardy as crafty manipulator was the administration's depiction of the Lower Covers.
His hundreds of supporters were elaborately pitied as hapless
dupes. They were "deluded, thoughtless individuals" who had

"too unwarily fallen into [his] snare." They were "unfortunate and hitherto deceived Loyalists," "unthinking individuals," mere "weazel varlets."[23] Even the Lower Cove candidates, if elected, would fall prey to Hardy's scheming. When Hardy appealed publicly for election of men of plain sense, chosen from the middling class, the Upper Covers responded that legislators drawn from such a background would become his "property," his instruments of faction. Another government supporter, noting that five out of six Lower Cove candidates were "bred to and have always been employed in humble tho' useful occupations," added poetically:

> An useful man in his *vocation*,
> In worst of times will serve the nation,
> While he *abides in his own calling*.[24]

In New Brunswick, governance was to be the work of independent gentlemen, not gullible mechanics.

THE LOYALTY CRY

When Attorney General Bliss and his slate circulated a handbill describing themselves as patriot candidates they also declared themselves supporters of "King and Constitution." In doing so they claimed an attribute that, they implied, their opponents lacked. While Lower Covers invoked the fearful terms conspiracy and slavery, government supporters broke the ultimate Loyalist taboo by branding their political enemies with the "odious and detestable appellation of Rebels."[25] A *Loyalist*, for example, charged that portraying a levy to participate in the lottery for town lots as taxation without representation caused him to shudder.

Such language was too reminiscent of propaganda circulated by the "restless spirits" responsible for the "late American usurpation."[26] A *British Subject* declared that the election offered Saint Johners "an opportunity of discovering their loyalty and attachment to government" by voting for the attorney general and his colleagues. Election of their opponents would prove to the world that "the seeds of sedition and rebellion are already sown."[27] According to *One among the crowd of Electors*, a Lower Cove supporter, pains had been taken to portray those opposing the election of the Crown law officers as seditious.[28] A *Citizen* — possibly Solicitor General Chipman himself — was even plainer. Hardy and his circle were "of a *republican craft*." Their principles "correspon[d] exactly with those of the rebels, by similar motives, or some caprice or accident, *flung* among the loyalists." They were "enemies of loyalty."[29] It was in the wake of this charge that the distressed *Americanus* included in his catalogue of "multiplied grievances" that his loyalty was suspected. He could not accept that opposition to Governor Carleton and his advisors amounted to disloyalty to King George and the British constitution, or that the only acceptable way Loyalists could show loyalty was by voting for government candidates.

THE CONTEST WAS VERY STRONG

The poisonous rhetoric of conspiracy and slavery, of sedition and faction, and the disorders, the prosecutions and the *Tumultuous Petitioning* law make it plain that the Loyalist experiment at the St. John River began in remarkable discord. What was the inner impulse that explains these three tumultuous years? The first historians to write about early Saint

John saw the tension as one between "aristocratic" Upper Coves and "democratic" Lower Coves. More recent writers have hardly deepened this analysis.[30]

Recollecting his Fort Howe days for an English audience more than thirty years later, the English journalist William Cobbett could still remember the distinctive labels the Loyalists gave their warring political factions: "One of the parties took the name of the *Upper Coves,* and the other of the *Lower Coves.*" On any map these two inlets appear close, but the Parr-town terrain was so rough that the easiest way to pass from one to the other was along the harbour shoreline at low tide. For this reason, from the very commencement of Saint John life, the population clusters at the two coves had the makings of distinct centres and rival hubs of commerce. Upper Cove was the more desirable location, and here the most prominent of those identifiable as government supporters held a great concentration of lots. Excluded merchants and artisans scrambled for commercial lots at Lower Cove. In this way there developed a distinction between the two centres for which geography alone does not account. Popular rivalry between the locales persisted for a century.[31]

Many Saint Johners saw their troubles in terms of a struggle between the patrician New Englander and the plebeian New Yorker. That's how William Cobbett, whose political instincts were first stirred by the contest at Saint John, remembered the parties. "The contest was very strong … The governor; the Law-Officers of the State; all those who called themselves the gentry; all the numerous persons in office, such as the Custom House people, and the like: these were of the Upper Cove party."[32] In opposition to them

Cobbett recalled merchants, shipbuilders and "independent and stirring lawyers," but he might better have described the inner circle of Lower Covers as traders and artisans led by lawyer Hardy and his Huggeford connections. In this sense the political tensions at Saint John did assume a colouring of exiles from New York and New Jersey resisting a New England-dominated elite.

In Cobbett's analysis, then, Saint John's political struggle was between, on one hand, a core of government appointees and a gentry whose former standing in the colonial world had been recognized and confirmed by Carleton's regime and, on the other hand, a core of upwardly-aspirant, self-made Lower Covers. The truth of this observation is confirmed by the many references to a class divide between the two factions. A 1784 defender of the Fifty-Five dismissed signatories to the counter-petition as mere "Carmen, ostlers, boys, &c," and lampooned the notion that its framers deserved to be called "Esquire." It was about the same time that the agents and directors drew a contrast between themselves as gentlemen and an upstart faction from barbershops and taverns whose "low birth" made them fit for only the "lowest offices in the state." Young Jonathan Sewell, one of the Massachusetts gentry, instinctively dismissed two of the Lower Cove "malcontents" in class terms: an "*itinerant auctioneer*" and a "*son* to the *keeper* of an *eminent grog Shop*."[33] Friends of the government greeted Hardy's appeal for election of men of "plain sense" from the "middling class" with elaborate disbelief and the stern observation that the lower orders should leave government to their betters.[34]

Had Willam Cobbett written his Saint John memoir closer in time to the events, he would have recalled another

sharp distinction between contending factions. The Lower
Cove leaders were Freemasons; Upper Cove leaders were
not. The pedigree of Saint John's civilian freemasonry is
rather complicated. It began in pre-Revolutionary Boston
with Lodge 169, the warrant of which was carried to Nova
Scotia at the evacuation in 1776 and then down to British-
occupied New York City. Among its members at New York
was Elias Hardy. Other brethren were Hardy's law partner
John Roome, Oliver Bourdett (later a close Hardy ally) and
one of Hardy's Huggeford connections.[35] Then in March
1784, when Hardy was in Halifax soliciting Governor Parr
(a fellow mason) for what became Chief Justice Finucane's
investigation of the agents and directors, he applied to Nova
Scotia's masonic grand master for the right to hold a lodge
at Parr-town. When formed, Hiram Lodge's meeting room
was at the Lower Cove, in John Kirk's tavern.

Among the seventy-four brethren admitted during Hiram
Lodge's twelve-year existence were at least thirty-five iden-
tifiably in opposition politics between 1783 and 1786.
They included four of six Lower Cove election candidates.
In contrast, only one identifiable government supporter
(Sheriff Oliver himself) was admitted as a Freemason, and
that was six months prior to the troubles. The occupations
of members is also notable. Eighteenth-century American
lodges of "ancient" masons, such as that at Saint John, were
notable for the broad spectrum of men they were willing to admit to the craft. In Hiram Lodge, merchants and
gentlemen were far outnumbered by a cast of artisans and
others of quite modest standing (stonecutters, carpenters,
tailor, watchmaker, printer, publicans, seamen, tanner, black-
smith).[36] When a government supporter charged that Hardy

and his circle were "of a *republican craft*" and "*levelling* disposition," the allusion was not just to Freemasonry (craft, level)
but to the levelled social standing of the brethren.[37]

In sum, political divisions at Loyalist Saint John were
coloured by class, sectional and geographic distinctions, and
these cleavages were mutually reinforcing. Yet it's mostly for
the score of men at the head of each camp that these factors
have meaning. The chief government supporters really
were New England gentry clustered at the Upper Cove.
Most leading dissidents really were self-made men from
the Middle colonies with lots around the Lower Cove. But
most likely there was not much difference in background or
politics between the six hundred opposition and five hundred
government voters. Put another way, the struggle for power
was played out between two contending elites. One was the
recognized colonial gentry — first the agents and directors,
then Carleton's regime. The other was a faction claim-
ing a share of that power. In the "boundless ambition" of
the Hardy-Dickinson-Huggeford alliance their detractors
claimed to find the source of all discontent. There is apparent truth in such a charge. Able and ambitious, Hardy and
his relations had been excluded physically from grants at the
Upper Cove and excluded politically from official power.
Even without the insight into their covert role in stirring up
dissent provided by the *Soldier* affair, their steady link to anti-
administration agitation from the end of 1783 until early
1786 reveals a determination to push themselves forward.
It was Hardy whose masterful opposition to the agents and
directors nearly brought them down. It was Dickinson,
presumably with Hardy's counsel, who headed the electoral
opposition at the 1785 election. Considering the power

wielded by Saint John's administrators, these near triumphs are impressive.

Essential though their role was in organizing and voicing dissent, Hardy and his circle did not create the anti-administration movement and did not control it. It had its origin and impulse in a factor more profound than a contest, however determined, between political ins and political outs. The wellspring of dissent was the sense of grievance felt by the whole Loyalist community after the decisive British defeat at the Battle of Yorktown. No one who studies the Loyalists in the 1780s can overlook the bitterness and despair that pervaded all ranks. They felt betrayed by their military in losing the war, then by their government at the peace table. It was this legacy of betrayal that fuelled the vehement reaction to the proposals of the Fifty-Five at New York in the summer of 1783. It is this sense of vulnerability to betrayal that accounts for the prickliness of Loyalists at Saint John — noticeable right from the time of the "blanket" protest at the arrival of the May fleet — at the prospect of receiving less in the way of public bounty than others received. It was the underlying source of their truculence towards the agents and directors, disposing them to see every shortcoming, every bias, every suspicion of favouritism as a fresh betrayal. This was the disposition of the whole mass of Saint John Loyalists, whether they chose to support the administration or the dissidents.

To take such a view does not minimize the fact that the exiles had a basis for grievance, but it does explain the persistence of an anger so great that it could still mobilize hundreds of votes for the opposition in 1785. Probably Hardy and his connections used this fear of betrayal for self-promotion both at pre-evacuation New York and again at Saint John. They may have channelled its politicized form away from Parr and towards the agents. They may have managed its re-emergence as an issue at the 1785 election, directing its force against Carleton's administration. But Saint John's sense of grievance was larger than Hardy and his circle. It is perceptible from the time of the May fleet, weeks before Hardy's role in the affair of the Fifty-Five at New York. It found forceful expression in Nathaniel Horton's company's catalogue of grievances, authored before Hardy's arrival at Saint John. The inability of the Hardy connection to control dissent is illustrated vividly by the Mallard House riot, where the crowd itself acted out a symbolic act of destruction at the headquarters of the Upper Covers. Most notably, Hardy and his relations could exert no control over the mass of dissidents in the wake of the Assembly's exoneration of Sheriff Oliver in January 1786. They did not participate in the great petition campaign of the following month. Presumably they advised against it. The powerful sense of "complicated grievance" felt by many Saint Johners at the fresh betrayals suffered in exile was beyond the control of its former leaders.

PERFECT TRANQUILLITY

In December 1786 the Anglican missionary at Saint John preached a masonic sermon before the town's most influential dissidents on the *Pleasure and Advantage of Brotherly Unity*. The sermon ostensibly referred to the fluctuating fortunes of ancient Israel, but George Bissett must have preached and been understood in a double sense. The "late calamities, owing to civil dissension" were the dissidents' own. So, apparently, was the "love and harmony" that now prevailed in the Saint John community.[38] In the short term, it seemed, political dissent was at an end. With truth Thomas Carleton could assure London that the "most perfect tranquillity" prevailed over every part of his province.[39]

But what of the future? Is there a sense in which Saint John's experience had broader political significance? The pioneering Loyalist historian Esther Wright saw such a link. In Carleton's successful campaign to suppress political dissent at the foundation of the province she saw the source of the "apathy into which everybody had sunk" a generation later. Her conclusion was that the "apathy, the stolid endurance, the preoccupation with getting a living" that characterized the colony of New Brunswick during its first half-century had its origin in the lesson taught by the election scrutiny, the *Tumultuous Petitioning* law and the sedition prosecutions of the 1780s.[40]

If Wright's conclusion is justified then one contributing factor must have been the departure from Loyalist New Brunswick of some of those whose vision of British liberty was incompatible with the most "gentlemanlike" government on earth. In the late 1780s there was a significant exodus to the United States and Upper Canada. By 1792 the population of Saint John had fallen to two thousand.[41] Dr. Huggeford and family were among those departing and he "wished he had gone Sooner."[42] Probably Tertullus Dickinson left as well. It's harder to generalize concerning the opposition rank and file, though the historian W.O. Raymond, reviewing the signatures to the seditious petition of 1786, noted primly that most were names of men who had left no trace in the province.[43] If this is so — that the exodus of the late 1780s included a number who had been active politically — then it may support Wright's theory about the longer-term political immaturity of the colony. The electorate had lost its capacity, perhaps greatly, to distinguish between loyalty to a united British empire and uncritical support for its local government.

Yet political quiescence was far from apparent in the New Brunswick of the late 1790s, when the colony's legislative process underwent a protracted political crisis. It was a late version of a common eighteenth-century American impasse: an elected assembly led by the brilliant Scots emigré James Glenie asserting what it saw as its constitutional privileges versus an appointed executive clinging to royal prerogative.[44] If the tempestuous politics of the 1780s had a relationship to what came later, surely it would appear as a link between the episode of Elias Hardy's opposition to Carleton's regime and the opposition led by Glenie in the 1790s. No one has ever found such a link. Despite renewed Lower Cove activity in the 1789 and 1792–93 provincial elections, there was no obvious transfer between earlier and later anti-administration alignments. Certainly there was no strategic alliance between Elias Hardy and James Glenie. Hardy had made his peace with Carleton in 1790, when he accepted the clerkship of Saint John, the post he had spurned in 1785. Then he retired from public life in 1795, the very time Glenie's forces were in their ascendance.

While these two political episodes seem unrelated if we focus on Carleton's opponents, if we ask instead why these crises occurred at all, a parallel does emerge. The Hardy affair of the 1780s and the Glenie affair of the 1790s became political theatre of grand proportion because the colony's governing circle chose to make them so. In each case Carleton's administration might have responded to challenge by resorting to political art. Instead it chose confrontation. In each case the ultimate weapon was undermining the legitimacy of its opposition by a charge of disloyalty. From this perspective, the crises of 1785–86 and 1793–99 become two effects from a common cause — the resolve by New Brunswick's governing elite to achieve psychological redemption through creation of a model Loyalist colony. Deviation from that model was resisted to the utmost.

The tactic used by Carleton's regime as its political trump card in the 1780s and again in the 1790s became known to later Canadian history as the "Loyalty Cry." When it felt its gentlemanlike vision of New Brunswick in political jeopardy, the governing circle equated support for itself with loyalty to king and constitution, and opposition with disloyalty and republicanism. Saint John was the earliest setting for a ploy that would have many echoes in nineteenth-century Canadian politics, and even later. A loyalty cry was invoked against nationalist *Canadien* politicians during James Craig's reign of terror as lieutenant governor of Lower Canada in 1810–11. It was a loyalty cry that smashed the reformers at the Upper Canadian election of 1836, triggering rebellion the following year. It was a loyalty cry that pushed New Brunswick voters to reverse their opposition to intercolonial union at the election of 1866, thereby making possible Canadian confederation. It was a loyalty cry that frightened Canadians away from free trade with the United States in the federal election campaign of 1891 and again in 1911. In different settings, in different generations, politicians would find the loyalty cry useful in undercutting their opponents because for most of their history British North Americans could not take continued independence from the United States for granted. Consciously or subconsciously, "loyalty" was almost always in question.

Yet on this original occasion, in early Saint John, the loyalty cry failed. Despite the regime's attempt to stampede the electorate by branding political dissidents as rebels, it was the Lower Cove candidates who, prior to the scrutiny, won a large majority at the polls, with almost universal manhood suffrage. In resisting the cry, the Loyalists themselves showed a self-confidence in their attachment to the British constitution that their children and grandchildren would lack. Ironically, the refusal of most Saint John voters to heed a counterfeit loyalty cry triggered only more overtly coercive measures as Carleton's regime went to extreme lengths to render eighteenth-century New Brunswickers passive and obedient.

NOTES

CHAPTER 1

1. P. Force (ed.), *American Archives: Fourth Series* (1839), II, 920.
2. The two aspects, desperate and chivalrous, of civil warfare around British-occupied New York City are explored in H.M. Ward, *Between the Lines: Banditti of the American Revolution* (2002) and J. L. Van Buskirk, *Generous Enemies: Patriots and Loyalists in Revolutionary New York* (2002).
3. Harding to Treasury, 8 July 1790: T 1, vol. 701; Statement of Parent's sufferings, n.d.: Saunders Papers (Military), University of New Brunswick Archives.
4. C.J.M. Sparshott, "Popular Politics of Loyalism during the American Revolution, 1774–1790," PhD dissertation, Northwestern University, 2007, 57–59, 67; Dibblee to Carleton, 31 Oct. 1783: British Headquarters Papers, PRO 30/55, f 9516.
5. *RWP*, 53n. The experience of other future exiles to the St. John River who fled to New York City on the same occasion is noted in R. East, *Connecticut's Loyalists* (1974), 25.
6. K. Cameron (ed.), *Church of England in Pre-Revolutionary Connecticut* (1976), 197–98; W.H.W. Sabine, *Historical Memoirs ... of William Smith, III* (1971), 136; East, *Connecticut's Loyalists*, 20; W.O. Raymond, *Kingston and the Loyalists of the "Spring Fleet" of 1783* (1889), 15.
7. G.A. Rawlyk, "The Federalist-Loyalist Alliance in New Brunswick 1784–1815," *Humanities Association Review*, vol. 27, no. 2 (1976), 142.
8. E. Wright, "The New York Loyalists: A Cross-section of Colonial Society." In R.A. East & J. Judd (eds.), *Loyalist Americans: A Focus on Greater New York (1975)*, 82.
9. Winslow to Barry, 13 Nov. 1778: Winslow Papers, UNB Archives; P. Smith, "The American Loyalists: Notes on their Organization and Numerical Strength," *William and Mary Quarterly*, vol. 30 (1968) 250, at 264, 266–67.
10. P. Smith, *Loyalists and Redcoats: A Study in British Revolutionary Policy* (1964), 77–78.
11. Billopp to Sydney, [1787]: T 1, vol. 654.
12. Ward, *Between the Lines*, Chs. 2–4; J. Shy, "The Loyalist Problem in the Lower

Hudson Valley: The British Perspective." In East & Judd, *Loyalist Americans*, 9; E. H. Tebbenhoff, "The Associated Loyalists: An Aspect of Militant Loyalism," *New-York Historical Society Quarterly*, vol. 63 (1979), 115; P. Papas, *That Ever Loyal Island: Staten Island and the American Revolution* (2007), 84–85 (victimization of John Bedell, Benjamin Micheau and Christopher Billopp); T. J. Wertenbaker, F*ather Knickerbocker Rebels: New York City during the Revolution* (1948), 229–31; O. Barck, *New York City during the War for Independence with Special Reference to the Period of British Occupation* (1931), 203–206. All paramilitary groups contained many future exiles to the Bay of Fundy; e.g., G.R. Vincent, *Civil Sword: James Delancey's Westchester Refugees, 1776–1785* (1997).

13. Barck, *New York City*, 177,182–83, Ch. 9; H. Onderdonk, *Revolutionary Incidents of Suffolk and Kings Counties* (1849), 186–92, 198; H. Onderdonk, *Revolutionary Incidents of Queens County* (1846), 157; Wertenbaker, *Father Knickerbocker Rebels*, 204, 219–20. There is an extensive Loosely & Elms miscellanea in H. Stiles, *History of the City of Brooklyn* (1867), vol. I, Ch. 9, pt. 2; also, *New-York Gazette*, 3 Mar., 7 Apr., 7 July 1782; [New York] *Royal Gazette*, 14 Sept., 16 Nov., 25 Dec. 1782, 9 & 30 Apr. 1783. A colourful view of life in occupied New York is offered in K. Scott (ed.), *Rivington's New York Newspaper: Excerpts from a Loyalist Press, 1773–1783* (1974).

14. S. Conway, "'The great mischief Complain'd of': Reflections on the Misconduct of British Soldiers in the Revolutionary War," *William and Mary Quarterly*, vol. 47, no. 3 (1990), 370; J. S. Tiedemann, "Patriots by Default: Queens County, New York, and the British Army, 1776–1783," *William and Mary Quarterly*, vol. 43, no.1 (1986), 35, at 37–41, 48; Papas, *Ever Loyal Island*, 90–94, 105; Memorial of John Fowler et al, 8 Jan. 1782: Raymond, *Kingston and the Loyalists*, 12; T. Jones, *History of New York during the Revolutionary War* (1879), II, Ch. 5.

15. Winslow to Wentworth, 9 July 1778: Winslow Papers, UNB Archives; Winslow on Clinton, n.d.: *RWP*, 65.

16. Carleton to Townshend, 27 May 1783: K. Davies (ed.), *Documents of the American Revolution, 1770–1783*, 21 (1981), 172; R. Chopra, *Unnatural Rebellion: Loyalists in New York City during the Revolution* (2011), 211-16; O. Zeichner, "The Loyalist Problem in New York after the Revolution." *New York History*, vol. 21 (1940) 284, at 286–95; Papas, *Ever Loyal Island*, 105-06; Information of Solomon Ferris, 11 Oct. 1783: CO 5, vol. 111; D.H. Villers, "'King Mob' and the Rule of Law: Revolutionary Justice and the Suppression of Loyalism in Connecticut, 1774–1783." In R.M. Calhoon et al (eds.), *Loyalists and Community in North America* (1994), 25; Informations of Isaac Foshay, Joshua Lamoreaux, Absalom Holmes, Daniel Babbitt and John Segee [May 1783]: British Headquarters Papers, PRO 30/55, f 7623; Wertenbaker, *Father Knickerbocker Rebels*, 259–60 (cases of Joshua Booth and Cavalier Jouett). An episode nearly identical to that of Ferris played out when Absalom Holmes, returning to Greenwich, was prosecuted for carrying off rebel property during the hostilities. Apprehended, beaten and taken before Patriot authorities, he invoked the peace articles. This they rejected "as he was Intended for Nova Scotia."

17. I.N.P. Stokes, *Iconography of Manhattan Island*, 1498–1909 (1915–28), vol. V, 1159; P. W. Coldham, *American Migrations, 1765–1799* (2000), 156; Feilding to Denbigh, 14 Apr. 1783: M. Balderston & D. Syrett, *Lost War: Letters from British Officers during the*

American Revolution (1975), 224; Winslow to Marston, 10 Apr. 1783: Winslow Papers, UNB.

18. Carleton to Boudinot, 17 Aug. 1783: K. G. Davies (ed.), *Documents of the American Revolution, 1770–1783*, 21 (1981), 208.

19. Loyalists did their best to collect precedents for financial compensation in *Case and Claim of the American Loyalists Impartially Stated and Considered* [1783], 26–33. Losses compensated were those attributable uniquely to loyalty, not merely the hazards of war, and only those sustained within the thirteen colonies. This latter qualification excluded losses arising from the invasions of Nova Scotia and Quebec, although a few claimants came forward anyway, notably five St. John Valley Acadians: Coldham, *American Migrations*, 806–09.

20. Botsford & Hauser to NY Agency, 14 Jan. 1783: [New York] *Royal Gazette*, 29 Mar. 1783.

21. General Orders, Army Headquarters, New York, 18 Apr. 1783: WO 28, vol. 9. The stringent one-year requirement was intended to confine the considerable benefits offered evacuees to bona fide Loyalists and deny them to mere speculators who might flock in from the country to seize the opportunity of bettering their condition in a new land. This occurred anyway.

22. [New York] *Royal Gazette*, 19 Apr. 1783; Lester to Carleton, 26 May 1783: British Headquarters Papers, PRO 30/55, ff 1966, 7952, 8008, 8013, 8274, 8346, 8615, 8973, 9070, 9152, 9255, 10111, 10123.

23. Ogden & Wheeler to Carleton, 2 June 1783: British Headquarters Papers, PRO 30/55, f 7872. Ogden was quite a character, avowing that no woman in equal circumstances had done more, said more, laboured more or spent more to support the Loyalist cause: Coldham, *American Migrations*, 308–09. (In exile Ogden and Wheeler would be allocated adjoining lots at St. John harbour, and they drew their building materials together from the commissariat.) Contrary to the supposition of their petition to Carleton, they required no special permission to take their own servants northward, who were victualled on the same basis as other evacuees. For offer of "a likely Negro Man" with clear title and well suited to the needs of a "family intending to settle in Nova-Scotia," see *New-York Gazette*, 21 July 1783; for another, see [New York] *Royal Gazette*, 9 July 1783. For an advertisement seeking "a free negro or mulatto bred-up as a tailor or capable of hairdressing and willing to emigrate to Nova Scotia," see *Royal Gazette*, 9 Apr. 1783.

24. J.W.S. Walker, *Black Loyalists: The Search for a Promised Land in Nova Scotia and Sierra Leone, 1783–1870* (1976), 10-12. White Loyalists were allowed to embark with their own slaves. Walker estimates that 10 per cent of evacuees from New York were blacks, free and unfree.

25. On Griffin: Van Buskirk, *Generous Enemies*, 174–75; F. B. Weiner, *Civilians under Military Justice: The British Practice since 1689 Especially in North America* (1967), 122–23. On Cairo and Pompey: Peters to Carleton, 5 Oct. 1783: British Headquarters Papers, PRO 30/55, f 9304; G. R. Hodges, *Black Loyalist Directory: African Americans in Exile after the American Revolution* (1996), 98, 159.

26. L. Sabine, *American Loyalists, or Biographical Sketches of Adherents to the British Crown in the War of the Revolution* (1847), 218.

27. Barck, *New York City during the War for Independence,* 214; Van Buskirk, *Generous Enemies,* 179–80; D. Syrett, *Shipping and the American War, 1775–83: A Study of British Transport Organization* (1970), 240.

28. Raymond, *Kingston and the Loyalists,* 12.

29. Captains' certificates: WO 60, vol. 23 pt. 1 & vol. 33 pt 1. Christopher Jenkins was deputy agent on the *Aurora,* Benjamin Anderson on the *Brothers,* Anthony Ferril on the *Camel,* George Leonard and William Tyng on the *Grand Duchess of Russia,* Jonathan Ketchum on the *Hope,* Ebenezer Foster and Richard Bowlby on the *Mars* and Andrew Ritchie and Thomas Gilbert Jr. on the *Spencer.*

30. The *Union's* two-week voyage between New York and Saint John was slow but not extraordinarily so. Press reports indicate that, while a trip up to Port Roseway/ Shelburne might take only a week, one to Annapolis or St. John River took longer.

31. Frost journal, W. O. Raymond transcription book 1: A 13, NBM. Frost's journal survives in Raymond's manuscript transcription but the accuracy of the excerpts he published in *Kingston and the Loyalists* is compromised by an effort at Loyalist myth-making. For this printed account he invented, altered and suppressed words and phrases so as to render Frost (his wife's great-grandmother) delicate and genteel for Victorian readers. Some of the strange history of the Frost text is sketched in G. Davies, "The Diary of Sarah Frost, 1783: *The Sounds and Silences of a Woman's Exile."* Papers of the Bibliographical Society of Canada, vol. 42, no. 2 (2004), 57.

32. *Clinton* muster book: ADM 36, vol. 9966. Variant nominal listings of the *Clinton* blacks are offered in Hodges, *Black Loyalist Directory,* 89–103, and Bell, "African-American Refugees to Annapolis Royal and Saint John, 1783: A Ship Passenger List." *Nova Scotia Historical Review,* vol. 16, no.2 (1996), 71. While I am uncertain how these particular companies were formed, army accounts at New York reveal that discernible parties of blacks contracted their labour monthly: e.g., Brinley, "Pay List for the Negro Labourers employed in the Fuel Branch of the Commissary Generals Department," 31 Dec. 1782: WO 60, vol. 31 pt. 1; Papas, *Ever Loyal Island,* 72–73; S. Schama, *Rough Crossings: Britain, the Slaves and the American Revolution* (2005), 113–16; Van Buskirk, *Generous Enemies,* 142; T.W. Braisted, "The Black Pioneers and Others: The Military Role of Black Loyalists in the American War of Independence." In J.W. Pulis (ed.), *Moving On: Black Loyalism in the Afro-Atlantic World* (1999), 24, 27–29. Perhaps these or similar groups were the germ of the companies bound for Nova Scotia. Victualling musters taken at Saint John indicate that the heads of the (eventually five) black companies were Stephen Hancock, Samuel Fleming, Richard Corankeapoon Wheeler, Daniel Haren and Lewis Carter. Wheeler, the only one not to sign with an X, is presumably the "Richard Crankapone" of later Sierra Leone history: Walker, *Black Loyalists,* 179, 243, 250. According to the army bureaucracy at New York, the Free Black companies to Saint John numbered 222 individuals, far more than the 132 who arrived on the *Clinton.* This seems plausible as in May 1784 the five free companies mustered 168, and probably others were now drawing as servants in "white" households.

33. Tyng to Watson, 31 Aug. 1783: WO 60, vol. 33, pt. 1.

34. *RWP,* 136–38; Petition of Elizabeth Hopkins, 12 Apr. 1816, in [Woodstock] *Carleton Sentinel,* 17 Sept. 1850.

35. *Camel* muster book: ADM 36, vol. 9430; Tyng to Watson, 18 Sept. 1783: WO 60, vol. 32, pt. 1.

36. C. Garstin (ed.), *Samuel Kelly: An Eighteenth Century Seaman* (1925), 90.
37. Tyng to Watson, 31 July 1783: WO 60, vol. 33, pt. 1; Knox to Winslow, 25 July 1784: Lawrence Collection, MG 23 D 1, vol. 24, LAC.
38. Unknown Saint John newspaper reprinted in [Portland] *Cumberland Gazette*, 11 Dec. 1788; Jarvis to Jarvis, 25 Oct. 1787: Jarvis transcripts, NBM. On 22 Dec. 1784 the *New Jersey Gazette* reported the recent arrival of seventeen Loyalist families from "Nova Scotia"; on 24 Mar. 1785 it reported thirty recent arrivals at New York; on 12 Oct. 1785 it noted that New Jersey "swarms" with returned Loyalists: Onderdonk, *Revolutionary Incidents in Queens County*, 256; Zeichner, "Loyalist Problem in New York," 296–301; S. Kermes, "'I wish for nothing more ardently upon earth, than to see my friends and country again': The Return of the Massachusetts Loyalists," *Historical Journal of Massachusetts*, vol. 30, no.1 (2002), 30.

CHAPTER 2

1. Frost journal, 29 June 1783: W.O. Raymond transcription book 1, A13, NBM.
2. Parr to Townsend, 26 Oct. 1782: K.G. Davies (ed.), *Documents of the American Revolution, 1770–1783*, vol. 21 (1981), 131.
3. Parr to Shelburne, 9 July 1783: Shelburne transcriptions, LAC; Parr to North, 23 Aug. 1783: CO 217, vol. 56.
4. Morris to Studholme, 5 Aug. 1783; Morris to Hauser, 1 July 1783: RG 1, vol. 394, NSA.
5. Morris to Studholme, 7 May & 2 July 1783: RG 1, vol. 394; Bulkeley to Studholme, 22 May 1783; Morris to Botsford, 16 July 1783: RG 1, vol. 136; NSA; De Lancey to Agents, 11 July 1783: Winslow Papers, UNB Archives. The Provincials were also allotted Musquash Cove and Quaco (poor tracts near the river's mouth) and formed the principal part of the grantees of Carleton, on the west side of St. John harbour. Provincials were also among the grantees of Parr-town. However, they did not receive any of the large river grants between Saint John and Maugerville.
6. Parr to Brudenell, [c. 1784]: Brudenell letterbook, Houghton Library, Harvard University; Parr to Sydney, 12 May 1784: CO 217, vol. 59.
7. For a view of the "intrepid," "vigorous" Studholme earlier in his career, see E. Clarke, *Siege of Fort Cumberland, 1776: An Episode in the American Revolution* (1995). His financial interest in the settlement process was confined to petty speculation in land.
8. Winslow to Watson, 10 Jan. 1784: CO 217, vol. 56.
9. Perhaps the earliest instance of the "agents and directors" speaking for and being recognized as spokesmen for Saint John Loyalists is Provincial Secretary Bulkeley's letter to Van Buskirk, Allen, Tyng, Leonard and Peters granting permission to lay out town plots, 22 May 1783: RG 1, vol. 136, NSA.
10. Leonard to Commissioners, 16 Dec. 1783: T 1 vol. 653.
11. The phrase appears in the charge against Arnold in Lawrence Collection, MG 23 D1, vol. 11: LAC.
12. Winslow to Marston, 10 Apr. 1783: Winslow Papers, UNB Archives.
13. "Description of the River St. John", n.d.: CO 217, vol. 56; Benjamin Marston, quoted in W.O. Raymond, *River St. John* (1910), 494; J. Bailey, "Tour of Nova Scotia, &c," [c. 1782–83], letter 13: Bailey Papers, MG 1, vol. 100, NSA; C. Garstin (ed.), *Samuel Kelly:*

An Eighteenth Century Seaman (1925), 91.

14. Inglis journal, 17 July 1792: Inglis transcriptions, LAC; Beamsley Glasier and Benjamin Marston, quoted in Raymond, *River St. John*, 359, 494.

15. Byles to Almon, 17 June 1786; Byles to Byles, 2 July 1787: Byles transcriptions, NSA; [New York] *Royal Gazette*, 9 Aug. 1783; Tyng to Watson, 20 July 1783: WO 60, vol. 33 pt. 1; Garstin, *Samuel Kelly*, 91; Williams to Watson, 16 Oct. 1783: WO 60, vol. 32 pt. 1; in contrast, Parr to Shelburne, 22 Mar. 1784: Shelburne transcriptions, LAC.

16. R. Morse, "A General Description of the Province of Nova Scotia...," [1783-84]: D. Brymner (ed.), *Report on Canadian Archives*, 1884 (1885), *xlviii*; G; Barclay, "Description of the Lands on the River St. Johns in the Bay of Fundy," 15 July 1783: Wentworth Papers, MG 1, vol. 939, NSA.

17. John Clark, quoted in *Raymond, River St. John*, 527; Peter Huggeford memorial, [December 1784]: RS 109, PANB; Winslow to Upham, [c. Aug. 1783]: *RWP*, 102; Garstin, *Samuel Kelly*, 90–91; Morse, "General Description", *xl*; Aplin to Smith, 6 Mar. 1784: CO 217, vol. 56; [S. Hollingsworth] *Present State of Nova Scotia* (1787), 112. Saint John always looked better from ship than land. One early visitor noted that, "[I] found that though the houses appeared pleasantly situated, from the ship, all seemed in disorder on a nearer inspection, for want of a good plan at first. It was with the greatest difficulty any man could be found, there being no regular streets or lanes. These hills were covered with small trees on their first arrival, and they grew so close that it was difficult to pass between them; it was therefore requisite to fell them, but by carelessly leaving the stumps six inches or a foot above ground, a person ran the risk of breaking his leg, or cutting his shin in passing through the settlement during the day. At night few moved from their habitation, as it would be difficult to find it on their return." Garstin, *Samuel Kelly*, 90–91.
However, within two years the town's streets, though unpaved, were said to be "extremely regular": [Charleston] *Columbian Herald*, 17 Mar. 1785. Saint John began cutting down the steep hills of Parr-town within weeks of the incorporation of the city in 1785, so that a modern visitor gains only a general sense of the original terrain: E.L. Teed (ed.), *Canada's First City: Common Council Proceedings, 1785–1795* (1962), 70; [Peter Fisher], *Sketches of New-Brunswick*, 42. On Henry Nase's house see Munger v. Nase, 1789: Lawrence Collection, LAC. A fair description of a settler's cabin at Sainte-Anne (Fredericton) is given in the "Narrative of Hannah Ingraham," in C.S. Crary (ed.), *Price of Loyalty: Tory Writings from the Revolutionary Era* (1973), 402

18. On fires: *Halifax Gazette*, 13 July 1784; Lamoreaux to governor, 16 Dec. 1784: RS 109, PANB.

19. By June 1783 some arrivals on St. John River had already planted potatoes and "sewed a great quantity of ground with all the essentials for their future comfort": [New York] *Royal Gazette*, 28 June 1783. This report was desperate optimism.

20. A New York Loyalist, Hecht lost property in that colony and another extensive property on the evacuation of St. Augustine. He was too poor to bring his family from England to Saint John: Hecht to Rose, 1 Feb. 1785: T 1, vol. 624; P. Coldham, *American Migrations* (2000), 156.

21. Allen to Winslow, June 1783: Winslow Papers, UNB Archives.

22. Tyng to Watson, 5 Nov. 1783: WO 60, vol. 24; Hecht to Brinley, 9 Nov. 1784, in Hecht

to Treasury, 12 Nov. 1784: T 1, vol. 611; Campbell to Treasury, 11 Apr. 1785: T 1, vol. 621; "Narrative of Mary Fisher": W. O. Raymond, "Some Notes Regarding Peter Fisher," in [Peter Fisher], *Sketches of New-Brunswick* (1825), 128. In contrast was the imaginative report of abundant fresh vegetables and cheap beef that one exile thought it useful to plant in the New York press: *New-York Journal*, 1 July 1784.

23. In 1784 a provision depot was opened at Sainte-Anne under William Garden. Until its establishment the Provincials clustered there had to draw from Fort Howe, 60 miles downriver. There was also a commissariat at Fort Hughes, a small post at the mouth of Oromocto River: Johnson to Fox, 28 Aug. 1783: WO 60, vol. 27.

24. *SJG*, 29 Jan. 1784; Polly Jarvis Dibblee, quoted in W. Brown, *Good Americans: The Loyalists in the American Revolution* (1969), 141.

25. Tyng to Watson, 2 July 1783: WO 60, vol. 33, pt. 1.

26. Beardsley to *SPG*, 26 Oct. 1784: SPG Papers, LAC.

27. [Philadelphia] *Pennsylvania Packet*, 27 July & 4 Oct. 1786, 26 Dec. 1787.

28. J. Beverley & B. Moody (eds.), *Life and Journal of the Rev Mr Henry Alline* (1982), 214; *RG*, 13 May 1784; G.R. Hodges (ed.), *Black Loyalist Directory: African Americans in Exile after the American Revolution* (1996), 73. Morris and Dibblee were from the same area of Connecticut.

29. Reece to Stone, 25 July 1784: Stone Papers, Archives of Ontario. The wet-nurse was Mary Murray, who was obliged in 1785 to sue Haws Hatch for 101 weeks care of his infant son: Murray v. Hatch, 22 Sept. 1785: RS 42, PANB; Jarvis to Jarvis, 8 Sept. 1788: Jarvis transcriptions, NBM. On masting see Munro, "Description of the River St. John's...," [1783]: D. Brymner (ed.), *Report on Canadian Archives*, 1891 (1892), 31; Douglas to Admiralty, 10 June 1784: ADM 1, vol. 491; Hecht to Treasury, 7 Feb. 1785: T 1, vol. 619.

30. Jarvis to Perry & Hayes, 21 Nov. 1785: Jarvis Papers, Shelf 86, F 52, NBM.

31. The NB Museum's copy of *Rules to be Observed by the Friendly-Fire-Club* includes a handwritten membership list.

32. Tomlinson to Stone, 18 Aug. 1783: Stone Papers, Archives of Ontario; Balfour to Wentworth, 24 Dec. 1784; Winslow to Wentworth, 26 Dec. 1784 & 5 Feb. 1786: Wentworth Papers, MG 1, vol. 939, NSA.

33. Byles to Byles, 12 Jan 1786: Byles transcriptions, NSA. The practice of making the queen's birthday a festivity was begun by the army at New York: J.L. Van Buskirk, *Generous Friends: Patriots and Loyalists in Revolutionary New York* (2002), 20.

34. Sewell to Sewell, 7 June & 3 Nov. 1790: Sewell Papers, MG 23, G II 10, LAC; D. G. Bell, *Legal Education in New Brunswick: A History* (1992), 2-3; M.E. Smith, *Too Soon the Curtain Fell: A History of Theatre in Saint John*, 1789-1900 (1981), 1-2.

35. Parr to Brudenell, [1784]: Brudenell Letterbook, Houghton Library, Harvard University; Tyng to Watson, 31 Aug. 1783: WO 60, vol. 33, pt. 1.

36. At the Sessions of the Peace for Sunbury County in May 1785, true bills were returned against five Saint John Loyalists, two of them women, for keeping disorderly houses. A year earlier the army threatened that those who kept "suttling houses, tents or wigwams" without tavern licences would be excluded "instantly" from the royal bounty, and their families also: SJG, 24 June 1784, quoted in W.O. Raymond scrapbook, vol. 3, 197, Saint John Regional Library.

37. In the case of Parr-town, where these earliest known allotments were made, this presupposes a preliminary town plan months before Paul Bedell's map of Parr-town, dated 17 Dec. 1783; similarly, lots in Carleton were distributed a year prior to Richard Holland's formal plan of 17 Aug. 1785. A fall 1783 arrival thought the settlements all in disorder "for want of a good plan at first": Garstin, *Samuel Kelly*, 90.
38. Sayre to Botsford et al, 25 May 1783: Botsford Papers, LAC.
39. Memorial of Peter Huggeford, c. Feb 1785: W.O. Raymond Transcription book, L. P. Fisher Public Library, Woodstock NB; R.C. Minette list of the grantees of Parr-town: MG 23 D7, LAC. Huggeford thought that the person chiefly in charge of lot distribution at Parr-town was George Leonard.
40. Land petition, c. 27 June 1785: RS 108, PANB.
41. Plain Dealer, in *SJG* 26 Feb. 1784; Huggeford to Governor, c. 24 Dec. 1784: W.O. Raymond Transcription book, L. P. Fisher Public Library, Woodstock NB; Winslow to Chipman, 26 Apr. 1784: Winslow Papers, UNB Archives; Tyng to Watson, 4 July 1783: WO 60, vol. 33, pt. 1.
42. Carleton to Parr, ibid; Morris to Studholme, 3 Nov. 1783: RG 1, vol. 394, NSA: Parr to North, 11 Apr. 1784: T 1, vol. 604.
43. Uniacke to Parr [c. 1790]: T 1, vol. 722.
44. Another controversy, over the size of blocks allotted to the disbanded Provincial units, arose at the end of 1783. This had propaganda value in the partition movement (as discussed in Chapter Three) but no practical effect in delaying settlement.

CHAPTER 3

1. Tyng to Watson, 25 May 1783: WO 60, vol. 33, pt. 1; Lodge, "Return of Necessaries Supplied...to the Refugees going to Settle in Nova Scotia," 27 Apr. 1783: WO 60, vol. 27; Watson to Tyng, 7 July 1783: WO 60, vol. 15. Loyalists would have regarded with suspicion everything that passed through the commissariat at Fort Howe as the army's commissariat department was notorious for profiteering and corruption.
2. Tyng to Watson, 25 May, 20 & 31 July, 26 Aug., 11 Oct. 1783: WO 60, vol. 33, pt. 1. Truculent refusal to labour for the common good was a characteristic of several Loyalist communities of resettlement.
3. Willard *et al* to Carleton, 22 July 1783; Carleton to Parr, 1 Aug. 1783: British Headquarters Papers, PRO 30/55, ff 8500, 8605, 10398. Soon a 56th name (Joseph Aplin) appeared: Carleton to Parr, 10 Aug. 1783: PRO 30/55, f 8682.
4. [New York] *Royal Gazette*, 9 Aug. 1783. The press reported that the committee for preparing the counter-memorial were "Samuel Hake, Esq; Elias Hardy, Esq; Captain Henry Law, and Mr. Tertullus Dickinson." Soon three of this group would be players in events at the St. John River. Roubalet's tavern on Broadway, where the petition lay for signature, was the meeting place of Loyalist New York's grand lodge of Freemasons, a brotherhood whose members would be connected closely with political dissent in Loyalist Saint John.
5. Tyng to Watson, 30 Sept. & 7 Oct. 1783: WO 60, vol. 33, pt. 1. The fleet carrying the Provincials had arrived ten days earlier.
6. "Proceedings of the 22nd Company of St. John's Militia," 28 Oct. 1783, in Parr to

Carleton, 31 Dec. 1783: CO 217, vol. 56; a version is printed in E. C. Wright, *Loyalists of New Brunswick* (1955), 82–83.

7. P. W. Coldham, *American Migrations, 1765–1799* (2000), 121–22; Cochran to Wentworth, 14 Dec. 1783: Wentworth Papers, MG 1, vol. 939, NSA.

8. Winslow to Watson, 10 Jan. 1784: CO 217, vol. 56.

9. Parr to Carleton, 31 Dec. 1783: CO 217, vol. 56. Probably Parr's misinformation concerning Hardy was a paraphrase of Gilfred Studholme's comments. As the account of Hardy is completely wrong, it is possible that Parr had misunderstood Studholme.

10. Sources for the pre-Saint John phase of Hardy's career include his memorial to the Loyalist Claim commissioners (AO 12, vol. 53) and testimony before the commissioners printed in A. Fraser (ed.), *Ontario Archives Report*, 1904, 217–18. Additional details are in [Williamsburg] *Virginia Gazette*, [New York] *Royal Gazette, New-York Gazette* and R.H. Kelby, *New York Marriages Previous to 1784* (1968). The Fredericksburg house in which he tutored is now a museum.

11. Alexander *et al* to the King, 10 Aug. 1782: K.G. Davies (ed.), *Documents of the American Revolution, 1770–1783*, vol. 21 (1981), 98–100.

12. John Le Chevalier Roome was an established New York lawyer who passed part of the revolution as secretary to New York's military commandant. He went to London in 1784 and may never have returned to America. Despite Hardy's differences with him over the affair of the Fifty-Five they remained partners in the scheme of gathering and transmitting Loyalist claim petitions to London for pay. They were also brothers in the same Masonic lodge.

13. [Inglis] "A Consistent Loyalist," *Remarks on a Late Pamphlet, Entitled, A Vindication of Governor Parr, and his Council* (1784), 17.

14. *SJG*, 26 Feb. 1784.

15. No copy of this *SJG* issue is extant. Edward Jack reprinted the *Soldier* letter in "Liberty of the Press in Parrtown in 1784": [Saint John] *Daily Sun*, 5 Nov. 1894.

16. Studholme had ceased to command Fort Howe after the reduction of the Royal Fencible Americans. Symbolically, however, he retained an office at the fort: *SJG*, 13 May 1784.

17. This was a serious incident in which a captain of the newly-arrived 3rd New Jersey Volunteers led an attack on sergeants and men of the Fort Howe garrison. Wounding several of the garrison's Royal Fencible Americans, the attackers took seven "prisoners" out to the transport fleet in St. John harbour, where most Provincial units were still waiting to land. Relations between the Royal Fencible Americans and other units of the Provincial military were tense because of the comparatively limited role the RFA had played during the war. As well, the RFAs were regarded as a predominantly Nova Scotia unit and Loyalists from the old colonies viewed Nova Scotians as half inclined to be rebels.

18. An Irish native, Eccles was formerly settled in South Carolina. Little is known of him.

19. On the senior Huggeford see G.J. Fisher, *Biographical Sketches of the Deceased Physicians of Westchester County* (1861), 28–29; P. Force (ed.), *American Archives: Fourth Series* (1846), VI, 152; Coldham, *American Migrations*, 259–60.

20. Parr to Nepean, 26 July 1784: CO 217, vol. 59. Parr charged the agents with delaying land distribution until (they hoped) the mainland was erected into a separate colony:

Parr to Shelburne, 16 June 1784: Shelburne transcriptions, LAC.

21. Aplin to Smith, 6 Mar. 1784: CO 217, vol. 56. Finucane's colonial career is examined in J.B. Cahill, "'*Fide et fortitudine vivo*': The Career of Chief Justice Bryan Fincuane," *Collections of the Royal Nova Scotia Historical Society*, vol. 42 (1986), 153.

22. The notice is mentioned in the "Petition" of the agents and directors: *RG*, 6 Dec. 1785. It was signed by Peter Huggeford, Oliver Bourdett, John Boggs and David Melville.

23. Leonard to Winslow, 30 Apr. 1784: *RWP*, 187. Three times Leonard refers to Dickinson as Hardy's brother-in-law; what he means is that Dickinson's wife Jane Huggeford was a sister of Hardy's wife Martha: E. E. Beardsley, *History of the Episcopal Church in Connecticut* (1868), 2, 195. Dickinson was from Dutchess County where he farmed and was a major in the militia before the Revolution. He "early became obnoxious to the Rebels" and was imprisoned at various places in New York and Massachusetts until, like Dr. Huggeford, he escaped into British lines in April 1777. He does not seem to have served in the Loyalist military. A former neighbour described him as "a Man of great Consequence and much looked up to, and it was known to every one that he from the first declared in favour of the British Government": AO 12, vol. 23; Coldham, *American Migrations*, 220–21. The Loyalist Claim commissioners granted him £740, less than one-quarter of his declared losses: AO 12, vol. 109. At New York in August 1783 he was one of the framers of the public protest against the petition of the Fifty-Five, along with Elias Hardy. According to a detractor, he reprobated the idea of resettling Loyalists in Nova Scotia until he arrived at Saint John on a trading voyage late in November, when he decided to stay.

24. Dickinson's charges and George Leonard's responses are printed in *RWP*, 180–84.

25. Winslow to Chipman, 12 May 1784; Studholme to Winslow, Sept 1787; Leonard to Winslow, 30 Apr. 1784: *RWP*, 186–87, 204, 346.

26. Leonard to Winslow, 30 Apr. 1784; Coffin to Winslow, 5 & 15 May 1784: *RWP*, 186–87, 203, 206.

27. Leonard to Winslow, 30 Apr. 1784: *RWP*, 186.

28. The earlier of the petitions, dated 13 May 1784, is printed in *RG*, 20 Dec. 1785 and the second in *RG*, 6 Dec. 1785; both appeared in print as part of the post-election attack on the Hardy faction.

29. NS Council Minutes, 31 July, 3 Aug. 1784: RG 1, vol. 213, NSA.

30. The ex-Provincials were Richard Armstrong (major, Queen's Rangers), Thomas Menzies (major, American Legion), Simon Kollock (captain, Loyal American Regiment) and George Dunbar (captain, 1st De Lancey's). Dunbar and Menzies had been objects of Tertullus Dickinson's charges of plural lot-holding but the disposition of the allegations is unknown.

31. NS Council Minutes, 31 July 1784: RG 1, vol. 213, NSA; Bulkeley to Hardy, 6 Aug. 1784: RG 1, vol. 136, NSA.

32. Several schemes for new or remodelled colonial governments in mainland America are ably summarized in A.G. Condon, *Envy of the American States: The Loyalist Dream for New Brunswick* (1984), 43–57.

33. Winslow to Chipman, 7 July 1783: Winslow Papers, UNB Archives.

34. The British aspect of the partition movement is sketched in Condon, *Envy of the American States*, 112–19.

35. Winslow to Chipman, 7 July 1783: Winslow Papers, UNB Archives.

36. Winslow to Chipman, 19 Dec. 1783: *RWP*, 157.
37. Winslow to Chipman, 26 Apr. 1784; Coffin to Winslow, 5 May 1784; Pagan *et al* to Hauser *et al*, 26 May 1784: *RWP*, 192, 202, 206.
38. Aplin to Chipman, 20 June 1784: Lawrence Collection, LAC; *SJG*, 13 May 1784; *Halifax Gazette*, 8 June 1784. Aplin was a busy, nervous lawyer from Rhode Island eager to ingratiate himself with the managers of the partition agitation. The Aplin affair was not Leonard's first use of rumour to subvert Chief Justice Finucane's authority. A week earlier Finucane had charged that Luke Thornton, Leonard's clerk, was circulating a report that Finucane had no "authority or power to redress any abuse or form any regulations whatsoever for the ease of the Inhabitants": Finucane to Leonard, 27 Apr. 1784: Lawrence Collection, LAC.
39. Parr to Shelburne, 13 Aug. 1784: Shelburne transcriptions, LAC; Parr to Nepean, 13 Aug. 1784: CO 217, vol. 59.
40. Parr to Shelburne, 16 June 1784: Shelburne transcriptions, LAC.
41. PC vol. 129: NA. New Brunswick's separation became official when, on Carleton's reaching Parr-town, his commission was read aloud in public.
42. *Halifax Gazette*, 7 Dec. 1784; Winslow to Wentworth, 27 Nov. 1784: RG 1, vol. 223, NSA.
43. W. Godfrey, "Thomas Carleton," in *Dictionary of Canadian Biography*, 5 (1983), 155-63.
44. [Philadelphia] *Independent Gazetteer*, 23 Aug. 1788; Inglis to SPG, 6 Nov. 1788: Inglis transcriptions, LAC; [London] *Political Register*, 13 Dec. 1817.
45. Early in his tenure Carleton walked to Westmorland. A few years later he walked all the way to Quebec to visit his ailing brother.
46. [J. Glenie], *Creed for St. John*, NB (1800). Not even W.O. Raymond could find much to praise in Carleton's public contribution: "A Sketch of the Life and Administration of General Thomas Carleton, First Governor of New Brunswick," *Collections of the New Brunswick Historical Society*, vol. 6 (1905), 439.
47. Hubbard to Peters, 7 Feb. 1785: Peters Papers, American Church Historical Society.
48. Sewall to Winslow, 10 Jan. 1776: *RWP*, 14; Chipman to Sewall, 9 July 1784: Sewell Papers, LAC. On the same theme, Chipman to Winslow, 6 June 1784: *RWP*, 209. The dislocation felt by Loyalists in England is a theme of M.B. Norton, *British-Americans: The Loyalist Exiles in England, 1774-1789* (1972).
49. Winslow to Chipman, 7 July 1783: Winslow Papers, UNB Archives.
50. Winslow to Watson, 10 Jan. 1784: CO 217, vol. 56.
51. *Aeneid*, I, 437; Winslow to Chipman, 7 July 1783: Winslow Papers, UNB Archives.

CHAPTER 4

1. *Halifax Gazette*, 7 Dec. 1784; "To the Electors": *RG*, 8 Nov. 1785.
2. R. Fellows, "The Loyalists and Land Settlement in New Brunswick, 1783–1790: A Study in Colonial Administration," *Canadian Archivist*, vol. 2 (1971), 5.
3. The decision was taken in Dec. 1784; a charter of incorporation followed on 18 May 1785: Winslow to Wentworth, 26 Dec. 1784: Wentworth Papers, MG 1, vol. 939, NSA. For the text of the charter see E.L. Teed (ed.), *Canada's First City: Common Council Proceedings under Mayor G.G. Ludlow, 1785–1795* (1962), 3–45; J. S. Tiedemann, *Reluctant Revolutionaries: New York City and the Road to Independence, 1763–1776* (1997), 26–28; G. W. Edwards, *New York as an Eighteenth Century Municipality, 1731–1776* (1917), Ch. 1. By the time of Saint John's incorporation perhaps three dozen places

in the middle and southern colonies had been chartered as cities but some had never functioned or had had their charters annulled. The remainder were a mixed lot, with only New York and Philadelphia as places of consequence: E.S. Griffith, *History of American City Government: The Colonial Period* (1938), 425–38.

4. Carleton to Sydney, 25 June 1785: CO 188, vol. 2; 14 May 1786: CO 188, vol. 3.

5. A specimen country charter (for Sunbury) is printed in G.F.S. Berton (ed.), *Acts of the General Assembly of Her Majesty's Province of New Brunswick* (1838), App. 3.

6. W. A. Squires, *History of Fredericton* (1980), 17–19.

7. *SJG*, 9 Sept 1784. The agents themselves had advertised some sort of history of their proceedings in *SJG*, 29 Jan. 1784, but no copy survives.

8. Huggeford to Carleton, [Dec. 1784]; Dickinson to Carleton, 28 Dec. 1784; Dickinson to Carleton, 26 Jan. 1785: RS 108, PANB.

9. Chipman to Odell, 25 Feb. 1785: Lawrence Collection, LAC; W. O. Raymond, *London Lawyer: A Biographical Sketch of Elias Hardy* (1894), 11. It was at this time that Hardy commenced his four libel actions against former agents and directors, as noted in Chapter Three.

10. *Loudon's New-York Packet* for 24 March 1785 reprints a florid account of the inauguration of the Supreme Court from a lost Saint John newspaper issue.

11. Carleton was instructed that, pending an assembly, "you are...to make such Rules and Regulations by the Advice of our said Council, as shall appear to be necessary for the Peace, order and good Government of Our said Province, taking care that nothing be passed or done, that shall anyways tend to affect the Life, Limb or Liberty of the Subject, or to the imposing [of] any Duties or Taxes.": W.M. Jarvis (ed.), "Royal Commission and Instructions to Governor Thomas Carleton, August, 1784," *Collections of the New Brunswick Historical Society*, vol. 6 (1905), 391, at 410.

12. Carleton to Sydney, 25 June 1785: CO 188, vol. 2.

13. T. M. Barnes, "Loyalist Newspapers of the American Revolution, 1763–1783: A Bibliography," *Proceedings of the American Antiquarian Society*, vol. 83 (1973), 217, at 230, 237–38. Sower's wartime career is outlined in "Applications for Half Pay on the Provincial Establishment of North America": T 1, vol. 608.

14. Carleton to Sydney, 25 Oct. 1785: CO 188, vol. 2. The franchise was confined expressly to males and to residents (thereby excluding non-resident freeholders), and the Council specified that "the votes of Blacks are not to be admitted": Odell to sheriff, 21 Oct. 1785, Lawrence Collection, LAC. The unexpressed rationale was that blacks lacked the capacity for mature political judgement. Moreover, to have allowed free blacks to vote while excluding slaves would have amounted to a sort of acknowledgment of slavery that might have been controversial. Acadian Roman Catholics were harassed in the Westmorland County polling and their votes became the basis for overturning the result: *RG*, 13 Dec. 1785; J. Garner, *Franchise and Politics in British North America, 1755–1867* (1969), 136–37. While voting by Roman Catholics would not have been illegal in New Brunswick, there being no election statute, many Americans would have regarded it as irregular (Catholics could not vote in New York and were banned or restricted in some other colonies), and for Acadians there might have been some question about whether they were natural-born subjects of Great Britain: R. R. Beeman, *Varieties of Political Experience in Eighteenth-Century America* (2004), 293-94. Catholic voting was challenged a year earlier in the general election on St. John's Island: J.M. Bumsted, *Land, Settlement and Politics on Prince Edward Island* (1987), 109, 146.

15. *RG*, 22 Nov. 1785; 6 Dec. 1785; Cooke to SPG, 17 Oct. 1785: SPG Journals, reel A-156, LAC.

16. The other Upper Cove candidates were Christopher Billopp (NY farmer), William Pagan (Scotland/Maine merchant and privateer), Stanton Hazard (RI slaver, privateer and trader) and John MacGeorge (Britain/NY merchant). The other Lower Cove candidates were Richard Lightfoot (mariner?, merchant and Freemason), Richard Bonsall (England/Penn. entrepreneur, Saint John merchant and Freemason in both NY and Saint John; in 1786 he was master of Saint John's civilian lodge), Peter Grim (NY tailor, Freemason), John Boggs (NC trader, privateer, Saint John merchant and Freemason) and Alexander Reid (merchant). The potential candidates not ultimately nominated were Stephen Hayt/Hoyt (Conn. merchant, captain Prince of Wales American Regiment; claimed to have smuggled 800 men from Connecticut to Long Island: C.J. M. Sparshott, "Popular Politics of Loyalism during the American Revolution, 1774–1790." PhD dissertation, Northwestern Univ., 2007, 71); John Smith Hatfield/Hetfield (NJ farmer/trader, notorious guerrilla: H. M. Ward, *Between the Lines: Banditti of the American Revolution* (2002), 58–59); William Wylly (Georgia lawyer, captain King's Rangers); and Elias Hardy.

17. On Massachusetts taverns as political space, see Beeman, *Varieties of Political Experience*, 77.

18. *RG*, 18 Oct. 1785; Raymond, *London Lawyer*, 9.

19. *RG*, 1 Nov. 1785; Odell to Oliver, 4 Nov. 1785: Lawrence Collection, LAC.

20. Carleton to Sydney, 20 Nov. 1785: CO 188, vol. 2.

21. On Halifax, Byles to Byles, 14 May 1788: Byles Papers, LAC. On Shelburne, Brindley to Watson, 8 Aug. 1783: WO 60, vol. 32, pt. 2; M. Robertson, *King's Bounty: A History of Early Shelburne* (1983), 128, 132–33; J.W. Walker, *Black Loyalists: The Search for a Promised Land in Nova Scotia and Sierra Leone, 1783–1870* (1976), 48–49.

22. Notes of evidence given at rioters' trial (May 1786): Lawrence Collection, vol. 21, LAC. Those who gave evidence were: (for the Crown) Christopher Sower, James Stewart, James Hayt, Sanford Oliver, Adino Paddock, Richard Seaman, John McKay, John McGill, Isaac Heddon, Robert Carre, Godfrey Leydick, John Carroll, Daniel Keefe, William White, William Hill, Thomas Billopp; (for the accused) Alexander Hackett, John Barrett, Elias Hardy, Thomas Kinney, Francis Watson, James Bell.

23. *RG*, 15 Nov. 1785. Although triggered accidentally, the attack on the Mallard House was part of a well-understood ritual of crowd violence in eighteenth-century America. Symbolically an attack on the headquarters of the Upper Cove faction served in place of an attack on the Upper Covers personally.

24. Those tried for riot were John Jenkins (guilty but recommended for mercy), Jeremiah Kean/Cane (not guilty), John Mullen (not guilty), William Riley/Reily (guilty), James Higgins (guilty) and Charles McConnell (not guilty).

25. See J.P. Reid, *In Defiance of the Law: The Standing-Army Controversy, the Two Constitutions and the Coming of the American Revolution* (1981); B. Bailyn, *Ideological Origins of the American Revolution* (1967), 61–65, 112–17.

26. For a U.S. account of the riot see [Philadelphia] *Freeman's Journal*, 21 Dec. 1785.

27. *RG*, 15 Nov. 1785; Carleton to Sydney, 20 Nov. 1785: CO 188, vol. 2.

28. *RG*, 22 Nov. 1785.

29. Charles McPherson's statement, 20 Dec. 1785; Dickinson *et al* to Governor-in-Council, c. 15 Dec. 1785: RS 60, PANB.

30. Protest of Dickinson *et al*, 20 Dec. 1785: RS 60, PANB.

31. In Britain and Ireland the economic influence of the military, particularly the Admiralty, in certain constituencies was considerable, but soldiers and sailors themselves did not vote. No instance is noted in L. Namier & J. Brooke, *History of Parliament: The House of Commons, 1754–1790*, I (1964).

32. A turnout of about 1,200 voters for Saint John County seems high given that it excludes blacks, but this cannot be proven. The population statistics in Teed, *Canada's First City*, 67, 70 are too narrow to be useful. Only slightly more helpful are the numbers in the "Return of Disbanded Troops and other Loyalists…receiving the Royal Bounty of Provisions, 31st Dec'r 1785": T 1, vol. 630. These indicate that about 1,100 adult males in Saint John County were receiving the royal bounty at election time but we have no idea how many other adult males there may have been. Another imponderable in calculating turnout is the Upper Cove charge that many Lower Cove votes were from men who did not meet the three-month residency requirement. Presumably this means that they were downriver from Kings County for the occasion.

33. Sewell to Sewall, 5 Dec. 1785: Sewell Papers, LAC.

34. Oliver's certificate, 24 Nov. 1785: RS 60, PANB. The Upper Cove candidates and thirty-three supporters signed the demand for a scrutiny.

35. Oliver to Dickinson *et al*, 20 Dec. 1785: *ibid*; Protest of Dickinson *et al*, 20 Dec. 1785: RS 60, PANB. As the Lower Cove slate decided eventually to boycott the scrutiny it is natural to wonder whether their decision was influenced by fear that the charge that many of their voters had not met the three-month residency requirement was well-founded. In one of their protests Dickinson and colleagues alleged that it was "mutually agreed by [all] the Candidates [before the election] with the approbation of the Sheriff, that three months residence in the *Province* should be deemed a sufficient qualification for a Voter." If the Lower Covers rounded up voters on this basis — bringing former Saint John residents downriver from their Kings County farms to cast votes for "impeachment" of the former agents and directors — then they would have good reason to undermine the credibility of the scrutiny by refusing to participate. However, in the extensive newspaper debate on all aspects of the election and its aftermath, this charge is levelled at the Dickinson slate only once.

36. The Council ruled that any irregularity in Oliver's proceedings would be sorted out by the new House of Assembly when it convened. It also said that, while it had not ordered the use of any particular election laws in the colony, yet "all Laws which are of a general Tendency, and whose effect must be to obtain an upright Representation, were supposed in Force, and therefore were not particularized…": NB Council minutes, 16 Dec. 1785.

37. Dickinson *et al* to Governor-in-Council, c. 16 Dec. 1785; Protest of Dickinson *et al*, 20 Dec. 1785; Statement of Charles McPherson, 20 Dec. 1785; Dickinson *et al* to Oliver, 22 Dec. 1783: RS 60, PANB. Sheriff W.S. Oliver's position as a government appointee sufficiently explains his opposition to the Lower Covers. The peculiar misfortune of being a Boston-area Loyalist must have made him especially wary of political dissent and those who stirred up crowds to riot. His father was the last lieutenant-governor of Massachusetts under the old regime. The father's "panic-stricken, remorseful, and dramatic" story of his experience as a prominent Loyalist is "perhaps the most vivid personal account of an official's confrontation with a mob of enraged townsmen and farmers in the literature of the Revolution": B. Bailyn, *Ordeal of Thomas Hutchinson*

(1974), 301n. For the sheriff's own war experience, see Oliver to Treasury, 7 May 1783: T 1, vol. 585.

38. *RG*, 3 Jan. 1786.

39. Oliver's return, 28 Dec. 1785: RS 60, PANB.

40. Some weeks earlier, after the scrutiny was demanded but before it had begun, a government sympathizer reported that: "Two of the professed Malcontents, finding that matters are likely to turn against them and that the powers of Government are strong enough to resist all their attacks, have this instant embarked in a small schooner for Shelburne from which place they sail for England. These *respectable personages*, viz Mr. Joseph Montgomery *an itinerant auctioneer* and Mr. John Keakwick *son* of the *keeper* of an *eminent grog Shop* are going from the factious party of this country in quality of *Ambassadors* to lay the grievances, ye weighty grievances, under which they labor before the house of commons, the house of Lords, the King, etc, etc, etc....Such are the romantic ideas of the New Brunswick Opposition." Sewell to Sewall, 5 Dec. 1785: Sewell Papers, LAC. Soon these two Lower Covers were back at Saint John, causing more trouble for the governing faction, if indeed they ever left. Judging from advertisements in the press, Joseph Montgomery had been a busy auctioneer in the waning days of Loyalist New York city before continuing that trade at Saint John. He was later jailed as one of the authors and presenters of the seditious election petition. Freemasonry records call him a merchant but trader seems more apt. Keaquick, master of the brig *Lovely Lass*, was also well-known through the New York press, carrying goods and passengers to Halifax, Shelburne, Annapolis and Saint John during the period of evacuation; one of his great nautical adventures is related in the *Port-Roseway Gazetteer*, 21 July 1785. Keaquick was mentioned above in connection with the Mallard House riot. One of his associates in the marine freightage business was Richard Lightfoot. Both were members of a militia company intended for Annapolis but both became associated with the opposition at Saint John, where Lightfoot was one of the Lower Cove election candidates in 1786.

41. 4 Jan. 1786: *RWP*, 323.

42. *Journal and Votes of the House of Assembly* [1786], 5–7.

43. Threat of deprivation of the royal bounty for misbehaviour, variously defined, was common in early Saint John. For examples, see Tyng to Watson, 20 & 31 July 1783: WO 60, vol. 33 pt. 1; Bulkeley to Studholme, 7 Oct. 1783: RG 1, vol. 136, NSA; George Leonard, 24 June 1784, quoted in article LXXXII, Raymond Scrapbook, vol. 3, Saint John Free Public Library; Hecht to Treasury, 7 Feb. 1785: T 1, vol. 619. During the election campaign the king's printer warned readers that the royal bounty was intended for the *"needy,"* the *"industrious"* and *"the Friends of Government"*: *RG*, 8 Nov. 1785.

44. All references to House of Assembly proceedings are drawn from its manuscript journal: RS 24, PANB.

45. Christopher Sower's statement is preserved in the Ganong Collection, NBM.

46. There were many American precedents for the house's proceedings, and the practice of forcing the offender to kneel and beg forgiveness also had colonial precedent: L.W. Levy, *Emergence of a Free Press* (1985), 18–19.

47. *RG*, 31 Jan. 1786. A government supporter responded to the address by demanding sarcastically, "Upon what principle must that commissary act, who receives a fulsome ovation, from George Shaw, Lawrence Dowling, James Conway, and Peter Grim?." Hake, a merchant at New York before the revolution, was a brutal, scheming liar who made trouble everywhere he went. He was ousted from the group planning

resettlement on Abaco. His Loyalist claim was disallowed for fraud and later his long tenure as Fort Howe commissary ended in disgrace.

48. *RG*, 14 Mar. 1785; Carleton to Sydney, 14 May 1786: CO 188, vol. 3. Neither printer was in prosperous circumstances. John Ryan was only twenty-four. Lewis had been jailed for debt at New York in 1783: G.E. Cullen, "Talking to a Whirlwind: The Loyalist Printers in America, 1763-1783." PhD dissertation, West Virginia University, 1979, 654–55. Within six months of his conviction Lewis was dead, after a "lingering illness": *New-York Journal*, 4 Jan. 1787.

49. *RG*, 21 & 28 Feb., 21 Mar. 1786; Winslow to Chipman, 21 Feb. 1786: *RWP*, 325.

50. J. Innes, "Legislation and Public Participation, 1760-1830," in D. Lemmings (ed.), *British and their Laws in the Eighteenth Century* (2005), 112–21; J. P. Reid, *Constitutional History of the American Revolution: The Authority of Rights* (1986), 21–23.

51. SNB, 1786 c. 58. It was copied from the Restoration statute of 13 Car II c 5 (1661); it is discussed briefly in Blackstone. The NB statute was repealed in 1854 and its English original not until 1986.

52. All references to House of Assembly proceedings are based on its manuscript journal: RS 24, PANB. Hardy's entry in the *Dictionary of Canadian Biography* errs in stating that he supported the *Tumults* law in the Assembly.

53. Press coverage of their trial identifies the four presenters as the petition's authors: *Loudon's New-York Packet*, 25 May 1785.

54. Both government supporters and dissidents saw Ludlow's refusal to grant bail and even to hear a *habeas corpus* application as harsh and extraordinary: Bliss to Blowers, 17 Mar. 1786: Bliss Papers, vol. 1603, NSA; Bonsall *et al* to Peters, 1 May 1786: Grand Lodge of Nova Scotia Collection — Hiram No, 17 records, MG 20, vol. 2001, NSA.

55. Arrest warrant, 8 Mar. 1786: Lawrence Collection, LAC.

56. Bliss to Blowers, 17 Mar. 1786: Bliss Papers, vol. 1603, NSA.

57. Dr. Huggeford, their father-in-law, who had figured earlier in the opposition to the agents and directors, was now in England.

58. Levy, *Emergence of a Free Press*, 11, 44–45; T. A. Green, *Verdict According to Conscience: Perspectives on the English Criminal Jury, 1200–1800* (1985), Ch. 8.

59. Documentation on the various trials is in case files for 1786 in RS 42, PANB. Hardy was counsel for the defence at the riot trial and at that of Lewis and Ryan. He was joined by Amos Botsford in defending the four presenters. The jury recommended John Carnes, a convicted presenter, for mercy, perhaps because of advanced age. As noted earlier, one of the rioters was recommended for mercy.

60. Carleton to Sydney, 14 May 1786: CO 188, vol. 3. Soon the governor would embark on a pedestrian tour of the southern part of his new colony, voicing satisfaction at the "content and industry that so generally prevails in that part of the province": [Shelburne] *Nova-Scotia Packet*, 31 Aug. 1786.

CHAPTER 5

1. E.g., the extensive discussion in *RG*, 15 Nov. 1785.

2. A cry against the Fifty-Five was also raised across the Bay of Fundy at Digby

in an election held at the same time as that at Saint John: e.g., *RG*, 27 Dec. 1785. This agitation, it must be emphasized, came more than two years after the plans of the Fifty-Five had been confounded, first by the counter-petition and then by Parr's unwillingness to depart from his official instructions regarding land grants.

3. *SJG*, 23 Nov. 1785, quoted in "To the Inhabitants": *RG*, 6 Dec. 1785.

4. Parr to Sydney, 26 July 1784: CO 217, vol. 59.

5. On anti-Massachusetts prejudice, see J.S. Tiedemann, *Reluctant Revolutionaries: New York City and the Road to Independence, 1763–1776* (1997), 199–200; P. Ranlet, *New York Loyalists* (1986), 3–4.

6. Many instances of politicization of section prejudice are given in "To the Lower Cove": *RG*, 8 Nov. 1785, and "To the Inhabitants": *RG*, 6 Dec. 1785.

7. E.C. Wright estimated that about 36 per cent of New Brunswick Loyalists were from New York, 20 per cent from New Jersey, 12 per cent from Connecticut, 7 per cent from Pennsylvania and 5.58 per cent from Massachusetts: *Loyalists of New Brunswick* (1955), 155–56. She thought these estimates for New York, New Jersey and Connecticut were probably low. The Massachusetts number is inflated by inclusion of Maine.

8. Bliss to Blowers, 17 Mar. 1786: Bliss papers, MG 1, vol. 1603: NSA; "A Friend Indeed": *SJG*, 13 May 1784; SJG, 26 Oct. & 23 Nov. 1785, quoted in "To the Inhabitants": *RG*, 6 Dec. 1785.

9. "To the Inhabitants of New-Brunswick": *RG*, 6 Dec. 1785.

10. For references to or extracts from Hardy's argument see "Mr. Printer": *RG*, 22 Nov. 1785; "To One amongst the crowd of Electors": *RG*, 29 Nov. & 6 Dec. 1785. This is about the only material of a political nature surviving from the pen of this central figure in the Lower Cove alignment.

11 For example, Jonathan Bliss, the head of the Upper Cove ticket, responded publicly to "*separate* and *distinct* objections against him as a candidate, viz. that he is a *lawyer*, and that he is his Majesty's *Attorney-General*": "To One amongst the crowd of Electors": *RG*, 29 Nov. 1785. The "No Lawyer" cry had become a staple of American urban politics. For its use in the Halifax election concurrent with that at Saint John, see Botsford to Chipman, 7 Nov. 1785, quoted in J.W. Lawrence, *Judges of New Brunswick and their Times* (1907), 177.

12 *SJG*, 20 Jan. 1784.

13 *SJG*, 13 May 1784.

14 Petition against the Fifty-Five [15 Aug. 1783]: Oversize 638, NSA; [Samuel Hake & Samuel Peters] "Gentleman of Halifax," *Vindication of Governor Parr and his Council, against the Complaints of Certain Persons* (1784), 24, 28, 31, 33; "Proceedings of the 22d Company of St. John's Militia," 28 Oct. 1783, in Parr to Carleton, 31 Dec. 1783: CO 217, vol. 56.

15 Carleton to Sydney, 25 June 1785: CO 188, vol. 2; Carleton's throne speech, 9 Jan. 1786: RS24, PANB; Winslow to Watson, 10 Jan. 1784: CO 217, vol. 56; Carleton to Sydney, 14 May 1786: CO 188, vol. 3.

16 Carleton to Parr, 26 Apr. 1783: CO 5, vol. 109.

17 Winslow to Chipman, 26 Apr. 1784: Winslow Papers, UNB Archives.

18 Jacob Bailey, "Tour of Nova Scotia, *etc*" [1783]: Bailey Papers, NSA; Cochran to Wentworth, 14 Dec. 1783: Wentworth Papers, NSA.

19 Leonard to Winslow, 30 Apr. 1784: *RWP*, 186; Petition of the Agents and Directors, 13 May 1784, printed in *RG*, 20 Dec. 1785.

20 *RG*, 15 Nov. 1785.

21 Coffin to Winslow, 15 May 1784: *RWP*, 206; "Mr. Printer": *RG*, 22 Nov. 1785.

22 "Aesop": *RG*, 31 Jan. 1786. This "weazel" motif in reference to the rank and file of Lower Covers also appears in "Mr Sower": *RG*, 21 Feb. 1786, and in Winslow to Chipman, 21 Feb. 1786: Winslow Papers, UNB Archives.

23 "To the Inhabitants": *RG*, 6 Dec. 1785; "To the Electors": *RG*, 15 Nov. 1785; "To the Inhabitants": *RG*, 15 Nov. 1785; Winslow to Chipman, 21 Feb. 1786: Winslow Papers, UNB Archives.

24 "Mr Printer": *RG*, 22 Nov. 1785; "To the Inhabitants of New-Brunswick": *RG*, 3 Jan. 1786.

25 Petition of Lower Cove candidates, 10 Jan. 1786: Ganong Collection, Box 36, NBM.

26 "To the Lower Cove": *RG*, 1 Nov. 1785.

27 "To the Electors": *RG*, 15 Nov. 1785.

28 "To One among the Crowd of Electors": *RG*, 6 Dec. 1785.

29 "Mr. Sower": *RG*, 24 Jan. 1786.

30 J. Hannay, *History of New Brunswick* (1909), I, 155; *RWP*, 323; S.D. Clark, *Movements of Political Protest in Canada, 1640–1840* (1959), 155–56; A.G. Condon, *Envy of the American States: The Loyalist Dream for New Brunswick* (1984), 147; W.S. MacNutt, *New Brunswick: A History, 1784–1867* (1963), 61.

31 W. O. Raymond, "The Town of Parr": SB 16, NBM.

32 [London] *Political Register*, 13 Dec. 1817, 1148–51.

33 [Anon.] *Remarks on a Late Pamphlet, entitled A Vindication of Governor Parr, and His Council* (1784), 17; Leonard to Winslow, 30 Apr. 1784: *RWP*, 186; "Petition," 13 May 1784: *RG*, 20 Dec. 1785; Sewell to Sewall, 5 Dec. 1785: Sewell Papers, LAC.

34 "Mr Printer": *RG*, 22 Nov. 1785.

35 Organized freemasonry arrived from New York in the fall of 1783 with the 57th regiment, one of many military (British, German and Continental) lodges in America. It was succeeded by Corporal Cobbett's own 54th Regiment, which also had an active lodge. H.P. Nash, "Origins of the Grand Lodge of New York," in *Transactions of the American Lodge of Research*, vol. 3, no. 2 (1939–40), 112. Lodge 169 included several members of the 3rd New Jersey Volunteers, who were dismissed in 1783 to form a regimental lodge: H. Whittemore, *Freemasonry in North America from the Colonial Period* (1889), 46–49. There is no trace of that lodge at Saint John.

36 S.C. Bullock, *Revolutionary Brotherhood: Freemasonry and the Transformation of the American Social Order, 1730–1840* (1996), 113; W.F. Bunting, *History of St. John's Lodge, F & A M of Saint John* (1895), 7–12, 16–17.

37 "Mr. Sower": *RG*, 24 Jan. 1786.

38 G. Bisset[t], *Pleasure and Advantage of Brotherly Unity* (1787), 5. The address was a St. John the Evangelist day sermon to Freemasons of the 54th Regiment. Typically civilian lodges also attended on such occasions.

39 Carleton to Nepean, 1 June 1786: CO 188, vol. 3.

40 Wright, *Loyalists of New Brunswick*, 149–50.
41 Chipman to Kemble, 25 Oct. 1792: Lawrence Collection, LAC; Byles to SPG, 24 Dec. 1792, summarized in SPG Journals, 15 Nov. 1793: LAC.
42 Clark to Peters, 4 Sept. 1790: Peters Papers, American Church Historical Society.
43 W.O. Raymond notebook 25: Lawrence Collection, LAC.
44 Sewell to Chipman, 6 Sept. 1789: Lawrence Collection, LAC; MacNutt, *New Brunswick*, Ch. 5.

FURTHER READING

The core of this book is drawn from three sources: records of the British army bureaucracy at New York and Saint John, located at the National Archives of the United Kingdom; records of the government of Nova Scotia in administering the St. John River region, held by the Nova Scotia Archives; and early Saint John newspapers available widely in a micro-film edition. On many points, more detailed documentation will be found in D.G. Bell, *Early Loyalist Saint John: The Origin of New Brunswick Politics, 1783–1786* (1983).

Readers looking to deepen their understanding of the Loyalist experience can turn to a wealth of solid historical writing. For the war period, Wallace Brown's pioneering *The Good Americans: The Loyalists of the American Revolution* (1969) remains a fine read. For the period of exile, Maya Jasonoff's success in weaving intimate personal accounts with the grand developments of the exile experience in eastern Canada, England, Jamaica, Bahamas and Sierra Leone makes *Liberty's Exiles: American Loyalists in the Revolutionary World* (2011) a minor masterpiece. It shows how the loyal friction that played out in early New Brunswick had striking parallels in other Loyalist communities. Many hundreds of individual Loyalists tell their own stories in Peter Coldham's massive synopsis of claims for financial compensation, *American Migrations, 1765–1799* (2000), though statements of loyalty and losses must be read with caution Two instructive studies of New York City and adjacent islands during the revolutionary crisis and long British occupation are J.S. Tiedemann, *Reluctant Revolutionaries: New York City and the Road to Independence, 1763–1776* (1997) and Phillip Papas, *That Ever Loyal Island: Staten Island and the American Revolution* (2007). Also useful are Philip Ranlet, *New York Loyalists* (rev. 2002) and Ruma Chopra, *Unnatural Rebellion: Loyalists in New York City during the Revolution* (2011). The contrasting faces of warfare — both chivalrous and savage — in the New York City region are captured strikingly in J.L. Van Buskirk, *Generous Enemies: Patriots and Loyalists in Revolutionary New York* (2002) and H.M. Ward, *Between the Lines: Banditti of the American Revolution* (2002).

A readable overview of the exiled Loyalists and the founding of what became eastern Canada is given by Wallace Brown and Hereward Senior in *Victorious in Defeat: The American Loyalists in Exile* (1984). New Brunswick high politics during the first Loyalist generation is the subject of A.G. Condon, *The Envy of the American States: The Loyalist Dream for New Brunswick* (1984). The best starting places for family studies of individual New Brunswick Loyalists remain E.C. Wright, *Loyalists of New Brunswick* (1955) and Bell, *Early Loyalist Saint John*.

INDEX

Higgins, James, 113, 171
Hill, Richard, 39
Hill, William, 171
Holder, Jacob, 32
Holland, Richard, 86
Holmes, Absalom, 160
Horton, Nathaniel, 39, 78-79, 141
Howell, Nicholas, 47
Huggeford, Martha, 81
Huggeford, Peter, 39, 81-82, 87, 107, 155, 168, 174
Huggeford, Thomas, 39
Huggeford, William, 87
Humane and Charitable Society, 62

Indians, see Malecites
Inglis, Charles, 64, 81-82, 100

Jenkins, Christopher, 162
Jenkins, John, 113, 171
Jouett, Cavalier, 160

Kean, Jeremiah, 171
Keaquick, John, 112, 173
Keefe, Daniel, 171
Kern, Michael, 64
Ketchum, Jonathan, 162
Kinney, Thomas, 171
Kirk, James, 65
Kirk's Tavern, 65
Kollock, Simon, 168
Knox, Thomas, 47

land issue, 68-73, 76-77, 78, 86, 104, 125, 135, 163, 166
  and tenancy/'slavery', 77, 85-86, 125, 140-42
Leonard, George, 20, 55, 69-70, 90, 95-97, 99, 111, 137-38, 144, 162, 169
Leonard, George Jr, 70
Lester, Elizabeth, 32
Lester, Sarah, 70
Lewis, William, 45, 83, 87, 109, 123, 125, 131-32, 174
Leydick, Godfrey, 171
Lightfoot, Richard, 117, 121, 171, 173
Loosely, Charles, 23, 110, 160
Loyalists defined, 7-8, 10, 15-16; 19
  military, 20-22, 30, 41
  morale, 25, 27-28, 58, 74, 123, 125, 152-53
  persecutions, 13, 16-19, 26-28
public assistance to, 20, 29, 31-32, 34, 36, 48, 52-53, 60, 62, 68-73, 75, 78, 84, 122, 161, 173

Ludlow, Gabriel, 104, 129
Ludlow, George, 100, 107, 127, 129, 174

McConnell, Charles, 171
MacGeorge, John, 114, 117, 121, 171
McGill, John, 171
McKay, John, 171
McPherson's Coffee House, 110-12, 123
Malecites, 50
Mallard, Thomas, 122
Mallard House, 67, 110, 112-13, 122
Mallard House riot, 112-14, 131-32, 138, 152
Marple, Northrup, 32
Melville, David, 106, 134, 144, 168
Menzies, John, 39
Menzies, Thomas, 168
Mercer, Hugh, 80
Merritt, Nathaniel, 42
Mersereau, John, 39
Methodists, 65
Micheau, Benjamin, 160
military and the constitution, 114, 115-16, 138-39
military units (British)
  7th Regt, 45
  17th Regt, 45
  37th Regt, 45
  38th Regt, 45
  40th Regt, 45
  42nd Regt, 45, 46
  54th Regt, 60, 113-15, 176
  57th Regt, 60, 176
  Regiment du Corps, 67
military units (Provincial)
  American Legion, 42
  1st De Lancey's, 43
  2nd De Lancey's, 43
  Guides and Pioneers, 21, 42
  King's American Dragoons, 35, 42, 57
  King's American Regt, 21, 42, 43, 60
  King's Orange Rangers, 46
  Loyal American Regt, 26, 42, 81
  Loyal Foresters, 56
  Maryland Loyalists, 43, 44
  1st New Jersey Volunteers, 42
  2nd New Jersey Volunteers, 42
  3rd New Jersey Volunteers, 42-43, 167, 176
  North Carolina Volunteers, 33
  1st Pennsylvania Loyalists, 42

Prince of Wales American Regt, 42-43, 87

Queen's Rangers, 43